Duck Hill Journal

Duck Hill Journal

A Year in a Country Garden

Page Dickey

FOREWORD BY LINDA YANG

Houghton Mifflin Company

BOSTON

1991

Library of Congress Cataloging-in-Publication Data

Dickey, Page.
    Duck Hill journal : a year in a country garden / Page Dickey ; foreword by Linda
Yang.
        p.   cm.
    Includes bibliographical references and index.
    ISBN 0-395-57783-7
        1. Gardening—New York (State)—North Salem.   2. Duck Hill Garden (North
Salem, N.Y.)   3. Dickey, Page—Homes and haunts—New York (State)—North
Salem.   I. Title.
    SB453.2.N7D53   1991
    635.9—dc20   91-15649
                            CIP

Printed in the United States of America

KPT   10   9   8   7   6   5   4   3   2   1

TO C. R. D.

AND THE CHILDREN

Contents

The Garden Plans

Foreword

BY LINDA YANG

No one who has overheard us each year still thinks it's funny. It must be a decade now, at least, that Page Dickey and I persist in our regular autumn routine. I ask (straight-faced, of course), "Can you spare some manure for my compost?" She replies (equally straight-faced), "I think so." And we chuckle as she trudges up the road to her three-horse barn, plastic bag in hand.

As the self-described "country mouse," Page gardens on several idyllic acres in a pastoral setting that is two hours by turnpike from town. I, now dubbed the "city mouse," tend less than a thousand square feet (or $\frac{1}{43}$ of an acre) between skyscrapers in a noisy metropolis. Yet despite the stark contrast in our landscapes, there's no end of sharing. That, after all, is the true gardener's way. That is also the raison d'être for this vibrant chronicle of a garden year at Duck Hill.

Here, in a smoothly crafted compendium adorned with her own watercolors and line drawings of flora and fauna, Page recounts in vivid descriptions her first-hand experiences, month by month, with an extraordinary palette of plants. These detailed records of garden species include the unusual and uncommon as well as the humble and unassuming. For she has tended a seemingly limitless roster of herbs, old roses, wildflowers, bulbs, and shrubs, woodland intruders, and roadside weeds. Page naturally harbors the dirt gardener's inevitable strong opinions and distinct preferences. Yet rather than create barricades of pedantry or dogmatic dictates, hers is a voice of gentle counsel that is encouraging not only to gardeners still unfamiliar with horticultural jargon but to those sophisticated to the point of being churlish.

How fortunate that Page has long been an inveterate chronicler. Surely the sundry garden diaries and journals so assiduously maintained for more than twenty-five years helped her hone her gardener's eye even as they now help her recall so many ephemeral pleasures and pitfalls.

I'm not sure how long ago I first heard her declare her own "passion for perennials." Certainly well before the current tide of fashionable interest swept over these shores. But it is only long-term experience that gives rise to such sensible suggestions as tucking lily bulbs among peonies so that the handsome leaves first provide scaffolding and later mask spindly fading stems. Witness, too, her effort to achieve that "fillip, a hint of sunlight . . . clear lemon yellow," which she deems invaluable for contrast in a predominantly pink- and purple-hued flower border.

With "no stalwart garden helpers at her side," there is her practical approach, too, to overhauling large garden beds: piecemeal, "a patch at a time." Advice to readers includes the note that such revamping need not necessarily be done according to calendar dictates of spring or fall but "when the spirit moves you."

I find uncommon pleasure in the sparkling bucolic asides.

Fascinating those roosters who "put their heart and soul into crowing," the ducks "standing on tiptoes . . . like ballerinas doing their exercises," and the geese hurtling along the driveway "with a racket of honking" in their nonsensical attempt to join migrating wild cousins overhead.

A voracious reader, Page is one of the few I know who refers so knowledgeably to legendary writers like Gertrude Jekyll or E. A. Bowles that she leaves listeners wondering whether she actually knew these gardeners in some previous incarnation personally. Yet steeped as she is in the wisdom of these British notables, she is distinctly American in her approach and a champion of the likes of Louise Beebe Wilder and Mrs. William Starr Dana.

In the rush of the modern world it is a relief to depart the highway that separates my city oasis from her rural knoll and maneuver the dusty, bumpy road that wends its way to Duck Hill. What a privilege it's been to watch these past years as she's brought magic to a site where few suspected such potential. I can only imagine the surprise of earlier occupants of Duck Hill's farmhouse were they to return and find the fragrant herb garden whose geometric patterns fill a window view beyond the kitchen table, or the billowing perennial beds with their splendiferous textures and tones, or an erstwhile gravel drive where four young crabapples now nestle in symmetrically positioned frames of boxwood hedging.

With her poet's ear, painter's eye, and disarmingly adroit way with words, Page makes it delicious to swallow whole even the most tedious of garden practices. Indeed, it is the purest of pleasures (paraphrasing Gertrude Jekyll) to linger in her Duck Hill garden for a year — if only vicariously.

Duck Hill Journal

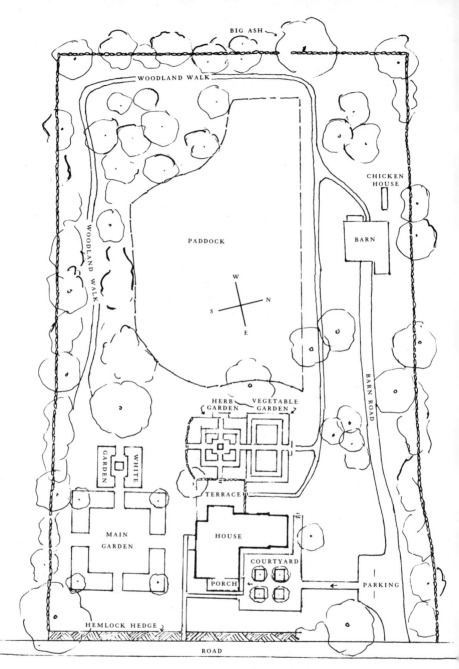

BIG ASH

WOODLAND WALK

WOODLAND WALK

PADDOCK

CHICKEN HOUSE

BARN

BARN ROAD

W
N
S
E

HERB GARDEN
VEGETABLE GARDEN

WHITE GARDEN

TERRACE

MAIN GARDEN

HOUSE

COURTYARD

PORCH

PARKING

HEMLOCK HEDGE

ROAD

PLAN OF DUCK HILL

Introduction

A round mossy space in a wood of hemlock and pine was where, at age ten or eleven, I decided to make my first garden. I remember laboriously lugging granite stones to line the path through the trees and more stones to edge the circle itself. Then I planted the circle with small wildflowers and ferns that I carefully dug up from the woods surrounding my garden on all sides. Why I was not satisfied to enjoy partridgeberry and polypody ferns and trillium where they flourished in the woodland all around me but felt I had to transplant them to a specific garden, I do not know. But I think of it now as the beginning of an enduring passion for making gardens.

Fifteen years later, married and surrounded by little children, I started gardening in earnest. It was the plants themselves that appealed to me, all kinds of perennials and wildflowers especially, their individual colors, their different shapes, perhaps the way they smelled. Being on a strict budget, but greedy to try each new plant that particularly caught my eye in a nursery or that was recommended in books, I tended to buy only one of each kind. The result was a hodgepodge of a garden, but I didn't care. I was happy growing my jumbled collection. It did not occur to me in those early days to step back and look at the garden as a whole, as a unified picture.

Then in the early seventies I bought for fifty cents at a library sale an old book called *My Garden* by Louise Beebe Wilder. It revolutionized my attitude toward gardening. Mrs. Wilder opened my eyes to the art of gardening, to the possible harmonies of color and texture and shape, "a gracious blending and contrasting of lovely elements."

This new approach meant simplifying my garden in a way, by growing fuller, bolder groups of plants. It meant seeing how the different plants related to each other, which combinations pleased my eye; and it meant trying to weave the elements of my garden into a unified whole.

Since those days I have read voraciously on garden design, benefiting from the wisdom and artistry of Russell Page and Beatrix Farrand, Vita Sackville-West and Gertrude Jekyll as well as Louise Beebe Wilder. I have learned to propagate plants from seed and divisions in order to have the bolder groupings that are so visually effective. And I have enjoyed attempting to paint pictures with my plants, sometimes successfully, other times not, always hoping to achieve a pleasing harmony in the garden.

About nine years ago, we left an established garden several miles south of here and came to Duck Hill, a three-acre piece of scrubby woodland and lawn around a small nineteenth-century farmhouse, sixty miles north of New York City. There was no garden, no flowers to speak of; no bulbs came up in the spring. Poison ivy and brambles covered much of the ground under a thicket of weedy trees — ailanthus, black locust, wild cherry, saplings of maple and ash.

To transform this into the Eden of my mind's eye was a daunting prospect. A limited pocketbook meant I would have to do all but the roughest work (chain-sawing, bulldozing) myself. I knew it would be years, maybe decades, before my garden was realized, before the slate was cleared, the bones of the garden created, the theme established.

The previous owners had left a small vegetable garden, and to this I brought bits and pieces of favorite perennials from my old garden. Here, too, I temporarily planted some old shrub roses — a collection that was my new enthusiasm.

That first summer and fall I prowled around our new yard, noting its assets, regarding the shape of the land, considering what to clear and what to save, watching the effect of the sun and the wind. I was grateful for the few ancient trees, maple and white ash, and the tumbled stone walls that edged our property. Some old billowy stands of purple lilac were a valued remnant from an earlier time. A few dogwoods graced the understory of the maples at our boundaries, and several single-flowered mock orange bushes bloomed despite the shade of overhanging trees and years of neglect.

I noted that we had sunny areas and shade, high dry land and low damp glades, meaning that I could grow a good variety of plants. I saw that there was some natural protection from the bitter west wind, for the house, typical of its era, had been snuggled into a hill, not built on top of it. But belts of shrubs and hedges would be needed to create a safer, more compatible environment for all the plants I wanted to grow. The soil, I discovered, was poor and sandy and only mildly acid.

About half of our land — the area farthest from the house —we immediately cleared for a barn and small fenced-in pasture; we had moved to this rural home in part to have a place for a few farm animals.

The rest of the property, all the land around the house and along the boundaries, was for me to deal with. I spent the first winter scheming on paper; it is a lot easier to move garden beds and trees and shrubs on paper than in reality. I knew I wanted a largish main garden with a mixture of plants— perennials, small shrubs and roses, annuals and bulbs, possibly a few fruit trees. I wanted a patterned herb garden similar to the one I had made and left behind, but more refined. A small vegetable garden was a must. So were some simple flowering trees and fragrant shrubs.

I wanted the gardens to be in keeping with the house, homely and old-fashioned, with many fragrant plants. Geometric patterns seemed correct extensions of the prim architecture of the house with its simple classical details; I drew axes from the various doors and planned paths to join one section of garden to another.

From the immediate garden area around the house, a walk was forged through our small stretch of remaining woodland, and here I envisioned a naturalistic planting of bulbs and ferns, native shrubs, and flowering trees.

Nine years have passed since that first winter of planning, and I have made some progress toward my Eden. Beds have been dug, and enriched with manure from our barnyard, and they now billow with shrubs and flowers. Evergreen and deciduous hedges have been planted and are beginning to form frames. Flowering fruit trees soften the lines of the house and give a sense of permanence to the garden. Hundreds of bulbs do come up now every spring. There is a certain feeling of unity, a sense of structure established, and the garden at its peak has an old-fashioned charm.

But there is much yet to be done, and years to wait before I have achieved the picture in my mind's eye. The dream and anticipation are part of the joy of gardening; the actual waiting to achieve that dream is some of its hardship.

For me, and for many people I know, the actual physical labor of gardening is a large part of its pleasure. I am never happier than when I am on my hands and knees, dressed in baggy clothes, caked with dirt, a baseball hat cocked on my head to shield the sun, my dogs by my side, the telephone out of reach, weeding my flower beds.

The following journal records aspects of a year in this maturing garden, its moods, its inhabitants (plant and animal), the discoveries made there, and some evolving thoughts on gardening in general.

January

Much is written today about gardening style, the latest fancy being the New American Garden, which seems to have a lot to do with grasses and rudbeckias and Easy Care. I am skeptical about the easy-care part, and I'm not sure I want miles of rudbeckia no matter how disease-free it is or how handsomely it blooms in August. And grasses are such a wonderful feature of the fields around us here at Duck Hill that I consider them less appropriate in a garden like ours than in a setting of meadows and marshland or by the verges of a pond or pool.

As I visit the gardens of my friends, I find that very few of them reflect this new American style, or for that matter are concerned with any particular garden style at all. Some gardens are formal in lines like ours at Duck Hill, others are naturalistic, with waving pools of flowers that follow the contours of the land. But each garden is completely different in look and in essence, an individual expression of beauty, reflecting the personality of its owner, his choice of plants, and his vision.

I cannot think of a colleague who talks about easy-care gardening. Someone who loves to cook does not think in terms of TV dinners and cake mixes and microwave ovens. This after all is not the point. Gardening is what we gardeners like to do: digging, fussing with our plants, weeding, deadheading — all the soothing creative labor that goes into the maintenance of our personal Edens.

It is exciting to realize that gardening is increasingly popular in America and that, consequently, every year a bigger, more diverse selection of perennials and shrubs and bulbs is available. More than ever, our gardens can be eclectic visions of independent-minded gardeners, as varied as is our vast country.

ON
GOOD
BONES

BARBERRY
(*Berberis thunbergii*)

It is this time of year, from December to March, when good bones really count in a garden. The eye is not distracted by leaves and flowers; it rests instead on the shapes and patterns created by our placement of trees, shrubs, hedges, walls and borders, ornamental pools, sundials, seats, and statuary. Good bones are a wonderful feature of English gardens, where ancient hedges and walls and avenues of trees are common and where a family is apt to maintain a design for many decades. Gardens with good bones are less common in America. We are more transient, rarely staying in one house for a lifetime, and gardening is not as much of a national pastime.

When I first started the garden at Duck Hill, I was anxious to establish its bones, or outlines, and this seemed most easily and inexpensively done by planting hedges.

Inspired by the magnificent yew hedges we had seen in England — deep and rich in color, impeccably clipped, and ideal as a background for flowers — I ordered several hundred baby yews from a mail-order nursery and carefully planted them in well-dug trenches around the main garden.

I had overlooked one thing: our deer population. Yew is caviar to deer, and Duck Hill sits in the middle of what is virtually a deer park, with no ha-ha or other obstacle between that park and our garden. Over the winter our baby yew hedge was eaten down to stubble. Undaunted, I replaced the yew that spring, and the following autumn carefully covered it with bird netting pegged securely into the ground. This kept the deer at bay until they realized they could eat right through the netting. After that I covered our infant hedge with wire caging for the winter but took it off in the spring. Then the deer took to nibbling yew all spring and summer long.

I have given up on yew hedges. Regretfully, I have replanted the outside of the main garden with the ubiquitous but relatively unpalatable privet. (I say relatively because deer seem to like any young twiggy growth and have helped me prune the privet by nipping off its tips.)

A neighbor and noted herb gardener suggested I use barberry (*Berberis thunbergii*) for the hedge around the herb garden, and so I did. Barberry is indeed considered a herb, for at one time the berries were eaten, the roots used as a yellow dye, and the bark dried for various medicinal remedies.

Planted as small cuttings, again ordered through the mail, the barberry is already full grown, very much a hedge. It is lively with brilliant red fruit in the fall and winter, and fresh green leaves and pale yellow flowers in the spring. The deer do not touch it because of its prickles, and even the chickens and ducks hesitate to barge through it in search of young greenery and bugs.

Nevertheless, I am not grateful for my neighbor's advice. Knowing what I know now, I would not plant a barberry hedge around a garden again. At least three times during the spring and summer my husband clips the barberry (clipping hedges is the one garden task he offers to do and obviously enjoys). A fast grower, the barberry hedge needs this much clipping to keep it from looking wispy, and I groan inwardly as I see all those prickly bits falling into the back of the herb garden beds. The thorns are lethal and soon become invisible, turning brown like the dirt that camouflages them. I wear thick deerskin gloves while weeding those beds, and I go about the work gingerly, but no matter how well I think I have raked up the clippings, I still get jabbed.

Barberry, unclipped, makes an attractive informal hedge, wider than it is high, and is quite suitable in a place where you don't have to work too closely on hands and knees.

I chose Japanese holly (*Ilex crenata*) as the hedge material to frame in the little white garden. It is a fairly good alternative to yew, dark green and glossy-leaved throughout the year, moderately slow-growing, and easily clipped. The deer do eat this holly in the winter, so we cover it then with wire, but it isn't one of their favorite foods, and during the growing season they leave it alone.

A hemlock hedge that we planted to conceal the garden

from the road has also survived the deer. They ignored it at first, but then one exceptionally snowy winter they developed a taste for hemlock, so now this hedge too gets a fencing of wire for the winter.

Hemlock grows quite rapidly and makes a handsome feathery hedge of large size and lively green color. It can be left to grow naturally, which it does with much grace, or it can be sheared, as ours is, once in early summer.

All these hedges, as they begin to weave together, emphasize the pattern of the garden; they form its outlines, enclose it, and give it some order. Never is this more apparent than when you look down on the garden from an upstairs window on a snowy day in winter.

SCHEMES

One of the pleasures of having a garden is scheming about it, and January and February are good months for putting these schemes down on paper. I keep a garden book in which I write notes all year long, recording what is in bloom when and for how long, what combinations of plants I am pleased with, and which need changing. I make note of plants that are deteriorating in health and need lifting and dividing or should be moved altogether to a more compatible place. I record the weather, its fluctuations and excesses, for this has a lot to do with what happens in the garden. During the winter months, I jot down ideas that come to me while reading books or going through catalogs or prowling around the sleeping garden.

Winter planning is the most fun when there is a brand-new area to be planted the following spring. I draw up lists of desirable flowers and shrubs, calculate the dimensions of the space, and then work out various ideas for a design on graph paper. The reality is never quite the way I have it on paper, but it is a guideline to set me going in the spring.

This winter I am making plans for the courtyard created by a wing we recently built onto the house. As I look out our north windows, this spot is now a sea of rubble and dirt and bits of wood left from the construction, but on paper it is already an ordered and flowery place. It will be our entrance way, enclosed by a clipped hedge (deciduous, I think, because of the deer), with gravel underfoot and brick-edged beds along the house walls. Four small trees (crabapples or maybe quince) will mark the way, like an alley, to the door. Where there is morning sun I will plant the fragrant daphnes (*Daphne caucasica* and *burkwoodii*) that bloom so tirelessly, the lovely *Enkianthus campanulatus* for height, some *Fothergilla gardenii* with its bottlebrush flowers, and a dwarf white-

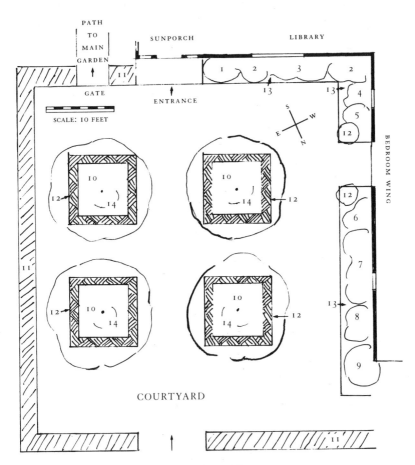

COURTYARD

1. *Pieris floribunda*
2. *Kalmia latifolia*
3. *Ilex glabra* 'Compacta'
4. *Mahonia aquifolium*
5. *Daphne* × *burkwoodii* 'Carol Mackie'
6. *Daphne caucasica*
7. *Fothergilla gardenii*
8. *Rhododendron* 'Waltham'
9. *Enkianthus campanulatus*
10. *Malus* 'Snowdrift' (white-flowering crabapple)
11. *Euonymus alata* 'Compacta'
12. *Buxus sempervirens* 'Suffruticosa'
13. *Hedera* '238th Street' (under shrubs)
14. *Vinca minor* 'Alba' (around crabapples, interplanted with *Narcissus* 'Jenny')

flowering rhododendron. Japanese andromeda and some new cultivars of our native mountain laurel will do well in the north beds, and I shall try the Oregon grape (*Mahonia aquifolium*), with its early scented flowers, and the graceful leucothoes. The four trees will be in small square beds edged in dwarf box and underplanted with periwinkle in which I will tuck bulbs of scilla or delicate narcissus.

≈

FROM
THE
COLD
FRAME

If I remember in early fall to plant a few bulbs of grape hyacinths and winter crocuses, daffodils and early tulips in clay pots and bury them in perlite in the cold frame, I am rewarded in January by the sight of fresh green spears and the promise of spring flowers. I bring the pots indoors a few at a time to be coaxed into bloom, knowing that more bulbs are waiting in the frame like some delicious winter grab bag.

This past fall, on a balmy day in early October, I did spend a few hours potting up some bulbs for winter. Having just read a book on miniature bulbs by Roy Genders, I was inspired by his example to try forcing a variety of these tiny early flowers. In four- and five-inch pots I planted a few each of snowdrops and *Chionodoxa luciliae*, winter aconites, *Scilla tubergeniana*, *Iris reticulata*, and *I. danfordiae*. Six-inch pots were filled with some of the dependable winter crocuses and grape hyacinths in blue and white.

A POT OF SNOWDROPS

I watered the pots and placed them in the cold frame on a bed of perlite, pouring more perlite over and around them to cover them well. I kept the frame open for a month, letting in all but the heaviest rain, then closed it for the winter.

Now, about twelve weeks later, I have started to bring the pots in to our cold sunny porch to gently force them into flower.

A tiny pot of snowdrops is blooming beside me as I write. It is merely a hint of what is in store for us outside in March when this first flower of the garden is in its prime. But how nice, in the bleak winter months, to have a miniature preview of spring.

❧

SNOW

A winter storm has left snow so deep that my legs ache as I walk around the garden, and Polly and Truff, our small shaggy white terriers, must leap like porpoises to keep up with me. The horses do not bother to forge through the snow, but stand instead by the paddock gate, their eyes closed, their lower lips relaxed and drooping, like old men drowsing in the sun.

It is amazing how a covering of snow instantly beautifies the landscape. Gone is the drabness of winter color, the shabby look of the ground. The light is brilliant. The old maples, etched in white, cast long blue shadows. Bushes weep gracefully, their differing hues enhanced by the whiteness. The dried field flowers and grasses are suddenly picturesque — cartwheels of Queen Anne's lace, disks of yarrow, and buff-colored plumes of goldenrod like bouquets in the snow.

The patterned herb garden is especially nice outlined in snow. The shrubby borders of germander and santolina and lavender still hold their shape and color. Round bushes of boxwood, richly green, punctuate the intersections of the paths. A sundial on its pedestal marks the center of the garden, and graceful bushes of old-time roses (damask, gallica, rugosa) give height and substance to its corners.

I am always startled to see our Pekin ducks on a snowy day. I think of them as white, plump and satiny white with orange beaks and feet. But against the snow, it becomes clear they are really not white at all, but a pale butter yellow.

❧

BOXWOOD

A pleasant task in wintry weather is brushing the snow off the boxwoods. Duck Hill's bushes of dwarf box (*Buxus sempervirens* 'Suffruticosa') are descendants of a friend's large dooryard bush, which she planted as a rooted cutting from Mount Vernon forty years ago. Amazingly, they survive our violent Zone 6 weather and flourish as long as they are kept free of snow and shielded from late-winter ice and sun.

I always cover the sides of our bushes with evergreen boughs sometime after Christmas. Recently a good gardening friend gave me a tip on how to secure the boughs. She advised tying soft twine around the bushes (baling twine from the hay in our barn is perfect for the job), then sticking the evergreens inside the string trussing. This keeps the boughs from blowing over in the first strong wind, and you can make sure the shrubs are evenly covered.

This little bit of care is well worth the trouble, for box bushes in the garden add an old-world charm and pungent fragrance that have no substitute.

FORSYTHIA

Sometimes there is a hint of snobbery among experienced gardeners, and certain plants are scorned as too commonplace to be included in their gardens. Forsythia is a shrub that elicits this scorn, unjustly. I know it is overplanted in neighborhood yards and often mistreated, sheared into dumplings or boxy

hedges, in the process losing its grace and most of its flowers. But who can deny its cheerfulness when in bloom in early April? And if allowed its natural inclination to fountain and weep, a stretch of flowering forsythia is a stunning sight.

The eminent plant collector Ernest H. Wilson writes in his book *Aristocrats of the Garden* that there is no yellow "purer or more vivid than the Chinese Forsythias." He reminds us that these are "sun- and loam-loving plants and are seen to best advantage when planted where they have lots of room and preferably on a slope, where they develop unmolested." He goes on to describe such a slope at his beloved Arnold Arboretum, where "there is a tangle of forsythias about seventy-five feet long and as much through and, as a feast of color and beauty in spring, is worth coming a long, long way to view." This was written in 1926; I wonder if Mr. Wilson's forsythias are still there.

Forsythia does not seem dull to me, as it is sometimes reputed to be, in other seasons.

It presents a fresh green all summer and provides an impenetrable and graceful screen. In autumn the leaves often turn coppery or purply shades and are handsome in bouquets with asters and chrysanthemums and sunflowers. In winter, too, the bush appeals to me, for the fountain of twigs is a warm reddish tan, particularly pleasing against snow.

But I would grow forsythia somewhere in the garden for no other reason than the pleasure of having branches blooming indoors, as they are now, when drifts of snow meet the windows and the temperature outdoors hovers around zero! Forsythia is the most obliging of flowering shrubs to force into bloom in the winter, requiring only a deep pitcher of water and good light. I cut my branches on days when the temperature rises to forty degrees, and can expect to have flowers a week or two later.

February

Amaryllis gracilis is blooming now for the second time in our kitchen. This and the more common hybrid amaryllis (correctly called *Hippeastrum*) are tender bulbs from South America that make splendid house plants for the dreary winter months. The large-flowered hybrids are seen everywhere before Christmas — at florists, gift shops, hardware stores, in garden catalogs. They have huge trumpetlike flowers with rounded petals in a brilliant array of reds, pinks, and white, borne on tall stout stems. *Amaryllis gracilis* is a smaller, more graceful plant that reminds me of the amaryllis in botanical watercolors by Redouté. The flowers are delicate and lilylike, with six star-shaped petals. They are a stunning Chinese red with a hint of yellow at their throats and pale-yellow-tipped anthers. Several flowers bloom on a slender stem and are enhanced by arching sword-shaped leaves. (A complaint of mine about the common hybrid amaryllis is that it often blooms before the leaves have expanded and looks rather naked and stiff on its long stalk.)

If the amaryllis plants are fed and watered and kept in the

sun after blooming, then given a short rest in the fall when the leaves have died down (put the pots in a cool place and don't water), they will miraculously come to life again in early winter with the gradual reintroduction of water and light, opening their bright flowers to warm us on the grayest winter days. *Amaryllis gracilis* is available in autumn from several of the well-known bulb catalogs.

ⁱ⁂

THE

SUN

PORCH

A sun porch was created when we built our new wing, enclosing what had been an open porch and our most commonly used entrance to the house. It is of modest proportions, with an entrance door at one end and long windows facing east and south. The floor is brick, impervious to muddy boots and paws and potted plants. The room is separately heated, and I keep the temperature low, around fifty-five. Here I am able to have a small winter garden indoors.

Most of the space is filled with a collection of rosemaries and geraniums (*Pelargoniums*, really), which thrive in the good sun and cold nighttime air. It is easy to get addicted to geraniums. Pots of the gaily flowered pink and red zonal geraniums are a heart-warming sight on a winter day. They can be easily persuaded to bloom all winter if grown from rooted cuttings started in May or June. (Four-inch stems root readily in a glass of water or in sand, shaded at first, then placed in an east or west window — it takes about a month.)

The fancy-leaved geraniums are a fascinating bunch, with variegated and splashed and zoned leaves of cream, bronze, yellow, and green. As though the leaves were not decorative enough, the flowers are also brilliant.

The scented geraniums are my favorites. They were discovered in South Africa by the English in the seventeenth century and brought over here by the colonists. Beloved by our Victorians, the scented geraniums virtually disappeared from commerce in the early part of the twentieth century. Happily, they are now enjoying a resurgence of popularity. They have a special charm, appealing to the nose as well as the eye, and it is hard, once you have a few kinds, to resist acquiring a collection of them. Grown for their leaves more than their flowers, their appeal (like that of a herb garden) is in their variety of leaf patterns and extraordinary scents.

The rose geraniums (*Pelargonium graveolens*) are probably the best known. Typically they have large, deeply cut leaves of bright green that, when rubbed, release a dusky rose smell. 'Mint-Scented Rose' and 'Lady Plymouth' are beautiful variegated kinds. 'Snowflake' has a round felty leaf, green splashed

ROSE GERANIUM
(*Pelargonium graveolens*)

GERANIUM
'VARIEGATED PRINCE RUPERT'

with white. Dried rose geranium leaves make a pleasant potpourri mixed with lemon verbena and lavender.

The lemon-scented geraniums (*P. crispum*) smell delicious, like lemon candy. Most of them have an upright habit of growth and make charming small topiary standards. 'Variegated Prince Rupert' is my favorite, with tiny crinkled leaves of green edged in cream and white. This little plant is a slow grower, but with patience it can be trained into an enchanting miniature tree. *P. crispum* 'Minor' is the fingerbowl geranium; in Victorian times the custom was to float its scented leaves in after-dinner dishes of warm water.

The peppermint geranium (*P. tomentosum*) is a favorite with children. It is fun to rub the large velvety green leaves to release the strong peppermint fragrance. *P. odoratissimum* is the pretty apple geranium, with small silky leaves, clusters of tiny white flowers, and a trailing habit of growth. It really does smell like apples. The nutmeg geranium (*P. fragrans*) looks similar, but the leaf is rounder and less indented, and the smell not quite as good. The filbert geranium (*P. concolor*) has small fuzzy leaves, deeply lobed and peppery smelling, with bright rose-pink flowers that bloom profusely in February and March. The oak-leaved geraniums (*P. guercifolium*) are quite different, with odd pungent scents and deeply cut dark green leaves sometimes marked with purple.

I often use the leaves of the various scented geraniums in small bouquets. They make lovely foils for snowdrops and miniature daffodils, roses and cottage pinks, and in the winter are pretty in a small jug all by themselves or mixed with some berries. They can be planted out in the garden beds in late May (when all danger of frost is past) and become marvelous fillers and ground covers among summer flowers. I take cuttings of the rose and peppermint geraniums in September to bring indoors — the plants will have gotten too big to dig up — but the smaller varieties can be lifted and pruned and potted for the winter.

If I am diligent about watering them whenever they seem the least dry, rosemaries flourish on the sun porch. I often wish we could grow rosemaries the way gardeners do in the south of England, as great mounded bushes outdoors all year round. In the Northeast, rosemaries must be dug up and potted for the winter months. Our reward, of course, is that their marvelous piny fragrance, rich green foliage, and pale blue flowers are a delight indoors.

The prostrate rosemary (*Rosmarinus officinalis prostratus*) is a profuse bloomer, lovely spilling out of a pot or trained into a weeping standard. The common upright rosemary (*R. officinalis*) makes splendid standards and is fun to train from unpinched rooted cuttings. The first year the developing standard looks silly — just a spindly stem trained and tied to a thin stake about eighteen inches tall. At first the leaves along the stem are left, but any growth in the joints of leaf and stem is pinched out. When the stem reaches the desired height, the top of the plant is pinched and pinched again (as new shoots develop) to shape it into a round head, and all leaves below this head are removed. (This is the procedure for training geranium standards, too.) By the second year the plants begin to look appealing — prim lollipop trees. In four years' time the heads are full and round, handsome now, on mature woody trunks.

In late May I take my standard rosemaries out of their pots and sink them into a bed in the vegetable garden, where they get a half day of sun. They seem to relish this vacation, and I am spared the worry and labor of constant watering. In late September I dig them up, prune the roots and heads, and repot them for the sun porch. During the winter months, about once a week I give them a shower of tepid water. (A deep sink in the pantry with a spray attachment does the job nicely.)

I am rarely able to pass through the porch without brushing my hand against the rosemary trees to release the heady, bracing fragrance. Rosemary is the herb of remembrance, a symbol of friendship, supposedly capable of clearing the head and warding off evil. The herbalist Gerard wrote that "it comforteth the hart and maketh it merrie."

COLOR OUTDOORS

Against the gray canvas of February, any hint of color stands out, pleasing my eye. In our nearby fields, wheat-colored now in the soft winter light, great tangled bushes of the multiflora rose have turned a deep wine red. Crimson buds are swelling on the swamp maples, creating a rosy haze among the tree-tops. The weeping willows seem almost in bloom with light yellow streamers. Clumps of golden pink grasses are echoed in color by the leaves of the beech saplings glimpsed through the woods.

I love the way the leaves of young beeches cling to the trees in winter like fluttering paper cutouts. If we had enough land, I would have a beech grove at Duck Hill. I often walked in one when I was a child, several acres of ancient gray-barked beech trees wound through with paths. In the fall it was an unforgettable place, a fairyland of pale silver and yellow.

GRAY
AND
WHITE
BOUQUET

*Abeliophyllum
distichum*

I have a charming bouquet of pussy willows and flowering *Abeliophyllum* beside me, arranged in a silver tea caddy — all white and gray and dark brown. *Abeliophyllum distichum* is commonly called white forsythia, but except for the shape of the flower, I don't see much resemblance to forsythia at all. *Abeliophyllum* (what an unfortunate mouthful this name is) blooms a little earlier in my garden, around the beginning of April. It is a graceful arching shrub, smaller and more delicate than forsythia. The flowers are tiny and pure white, borne in tight clusters on pale stems. They expand from dark brown buds to pale yellow unopened flowers tinged with pink, then open to four-petaled white stars with tiny golden stamens. The flowers smell sweetly of honey. In full bloom, *Abeliophyllum* is a pretty sight, especially on an overcast day or against an evergreen background. The branches can be easily forced into flower in February and March, and in early April are lovely in bouquets with the first trumpet daffodils.

I have planted three different kinds of pussy willows at Duck Hill — something childish in me loves the sight of those silvery catkins opening now in wet meadows and along roadsides. I have always wanted my own to admire and touch and cut for vases indoors.

I have not included in Duck Hill's collection our native pussy willow (*Salix discolor*), for it flourishes in the adjacent fields where I walk daily with our dogs. It is a large upright shrub with broad green leaves that shade to white on their undersides. The silver-white pussies, so delightful to see shimmering against a blue sky, open from shiny chocolate-brown scales on gray-brown stems. A month later they expand into fluffy flowers of the palest yellow-green.

Salix caprea, the French pussy willow or goat willow, is the one most often sold by florists. It also grows into a big bush and has greenish brown stems and large plump silvery catkins. *S. gracilistyla* is a smaller shrub with woolly stems and appealing catkins that start out gray and silky, then become flushed with pink, finally expanding to yellow. *S.* 'Melanostachys' is an odd and striking pussy willow, low-growing, glossy-leaved, with red stems and small black catkins showing red anthers as they mature.

The pussy willows are planted near the barn where it is

moist and sunny. Here their summer greenness is appreciated, and if the Japanese beetles discover them (the leaves appear to be a favorite food), I am not too concerned. Deer also love to eat the tips of the young bushes, so in winter I protect them with netting or wire.

VERNAL
WITCH
HAZEL

SPRING
FEVER

Invariably, near the end of February there is a spell of warm weather that makes us think of spring. We shed our hats and coats and wander about listening to the bird's song and inhaling the smell of wet earth. The barn doors are opened wide; the horses, unblanketed, roll in the mud. The geese and ducks stray far beyond the barnyard in their search for bugs, stopping only to try each puddle, bellies low, scooping their heads to let the muddy water roll down their necks and backs.

Our roosters, usually content to coexist with their separate bevies of hens, feel spring stirring and start a cockfight. It reminds me, in its formality, of a fencing duel. The two roosters stand off and face each other, ruffs fully extended, exposing their scrawny necks. They stare at each other fiercely and then in unison leap together in the air, striking at each other with their spurred legs. A second later they back off and formally face each other again. The standing and striking continue as they twirl around the barnyard until finally one of the roosters turns to run, with the other in full chase. The hens stand watching along with me, clucking quietly.

Snowdrops are in bud along the woodland path, and the vernal witch hazel begins to bloom — tiny tassels of burnished red.

March

SNOWDROPS

Acquaintances sometimes ask me what my favorite flower is, and I have no answer. I could not single out one flower above all others. But the question starts me musing about the flowers that I would put at the top of my list. Certainly roses would be there, the sweet-scented old-fashioned ones, and the entire *Viola* family (violets, Johnny-jump-ups, pansies, and violas). All kinds of daffodils would have to be included, and the snowdrop, that harbinger of spring for which I have always felt a special affection.

Unless we have had a deep snow, I can count on having snowdrops in bloom by the first week in March, and what a thrill it is to find these first flowers of the year! Two swordlike leaves push through winter's frozen ground and debris and unclasp the pendent buds — glistening white teardrops that dangle by threads from their slender stems. They are not at all the fragile flowers they seem, surviving through weeks of volatile March weather, with its spells of snow and ice and lashing rain. As the weather softens, the three outer petals, or segments, of the flower flare open and reveal an inner bell (really three overlapping segments) delicately scalloped and notched with green.

Clumps and drifts of the common snowdrop (*Galanthus nivalis*) flourish along our ribbon of woods in the light shade of deciduous trees and shrubs. On soft damp days, when I walk down the path to see the patches of green and white, I catch whiffs of their marvelous honey fragrance.

We have one fat clump of double snowdrops (*G. nivalis* 'Flore Pleno') that I find endearing, although they have none of the grace of the single snowdrop. Their outer petals are pushed open by a series of bulging inner bells that look like green-trimmed white crinolines.

G. elwesii is a larger snowdrop, taller-growing, with broad gray-green leaves. It does not increase like the common snowdrop, but it has the advantage of blooming a week or two earlier than *G. nivalis*, thus bringing spring to us that much sooner.

That charming Edwardian gardener E. A. Bowles, writing in the early 1900s in England, describes many other varieties of snowdrops blooming from late October until April. And Louise Beebe Wilder, our own great garden writer of those early decades, mentions almost two dozen kinds. But I have yet to find in a current American catalog any snowdrops other than those I have growing at Duck Hill.

A few flowers of any of these snowdrops, cut and mixed with some leaves of scented geraniums or early sprigs of greater celandine and tansy, make a fragrant posy for a tiny vase.

When the snowdrops start to fade, I like to dig up one of the older clumps and gently pull it apart, replanting some of the bulbs in the same spot, to which I have added some compost. With the other bulbs in a basket and a trowel in hand, I walk up the woodland path eyeing other places where snowdrops might be planted, then tuck them in with a trowelful of compost. This method of propagation seems to work well, although with no effort at all on my part the bulbs do increase and seed around. I look forward to the time when there are sheets of snowdrops as far as the eye can travel through our little woodland.

᳁

THE
FIRST
YELLOWS

I am invariably surprised one sunny day around the beginning of March to discover the cheerful cream and golden goblets of *Crocus chrysanthus* wide open in sheltered places near the house. The bees have discovered them before me and are humming busily around their bright orange stigmata.

These small, early-flowering crocuses quickly multiply into clotted clumps and are the first real splash of color in the garden. But it is only on soft sunlit days that they are persuaded to open and reveal the brilliance of their color. The outside segments of the flowers are usually feathered and colored with a duller hue, and in chilly weather the crocuses remain tightly shut. Their display is sometimes short-lived for, not having the strong constitution of snowdrops, they can be battered by hard-driving rain or snow. Nevertheless, their fleeting cheerfulness is worth the small bit of effort it takes in the fall to plant the tiny corms around shrubs and long-lived perennials near the house.

'Goldilocks', 'Cream Beauty', and 'E. A. Bowles' are the yellow varieties that bloom here first, but *C. chrysanthus* also comes in white and lavender and purple. One kind planted in our terrace beds is called 'Lady Killer' (surely a better name could have been found for a small white crocus). The flower is pure white inside, spiked by orange stigmata; outside, the petals are broadly feathered in purple. Two other species of crocuses bloom with *C. chrysanthus* in my garden and spread freely into drifts in a few years: *C. sieberi*, gray-clothed in bud but a luminous lavender when open, and *C. tomasinianus*, a delicate flower of pale amethyst.

Winter aconites (*Eranthis hyemalis*) closely follow the earliest crocuses and snowdrops. They open from small golden balls to buttercup blooms that rest on ruffs of deeply cut greenery. They enjoy the same situation as snowdrops, and the two flowers, yellow and white, blooming together, are a pleasing picture. Winter aconites increase slowly but steadily, and I am always heartened to see the pretty, palmately cut leaves of seedlings around established clumps, promising a few more blooms each year.

WINTER ACONITE
(*Eranthis hyemalis*)

NAKED JASMINE
(*Jasminum nudiflorum*)

By the middle of March, naked jasmine (*Jasminum nudiflorum*) begins to open its yellow stars. This is an appealing vine (or lax shrub) to train against or spill from a south wall, providing a sunny display for several weeks. The flowers, bright butter yellow, are similar to those of forsythia but with six petals instead of four and rounder in shape, opening from red-tinged buds.

Here at Duck Hill, sprays of naked jasmine clothe the southeast side of a low stone wall that borders our terrace. The early yellow flowers look particularly fine against the gray stone. They are a gladdening sight on chilly days as we walk from the kitchen door to the barn and back.

After the jasmine has finished flowering, I clip it back fairly hard. I find this ensures good bloom for the following year and keeps it from sprawling too much. Wherever the branches touch the ground they root, affording plenty of small plants to use elsewhere or give away to friends.

፠

SOME
PRUNING

Without fail, sometime early in March we have a delicious
stretch of warm weather (temperatures in the sixties and
seventies, soft sun, damp earthy smell) when, if my chores
are done and I have no other pressing commitments, nothing
can induce me to stay indoors. But the lawn and garden beds
are wet, the gravel paths squishy underfoot, so I busy myself
with some pruning.

I tackle the raspberries, cutting all last year's fruiting canes
down to the ground (I could do this in the fall, but I feel lazy
then) and shearing back the new unbranched canes to about
three feet.

The purple smokebush (*Cotinus coggygria* 'Royal Purple'),
which billows by the arbor that leads into the vegetable garden, gets a good cropping; I cut back much of last year's
growth to keep it from getting too large and out of scale.

I stare hard at the great free-standing clumps of forsythia
to see if there is any old unproductive wood to cut out at the
base; if so, I do it now with my pruning saw, knowing that in
late April (when one is advised to prune forsythia) I will be
too busy in the garden to tend to this.

I go over the mock orange bushes (varieties of *Philadelphus*), cutting out any dead twiggy growth and carefully
stacking it, for these branches make marvelous stakes in the
garden. I use the stouter ones to hold up fountains of roses
and put the smaller, twiggier branches among perennials that
are apt to loll and sag.

The variegated red-stemmed dogwoods (*Cornus alba* 'Elegantissima') get a pruning (I cut the branches back by half) to encourage new growth, which will be the brightest red next winter. I bring the trimmed branches indoors to coax into leaf and flower in warm water. The forced leaves are not as large as they would be outdoors but are nonetheless effective — a fresh light green edged in white.

If I cut a few graceful twigs of the single-flowered bright yellow *Kerria japonica* while clearing this good shrub of any deadwood, these can also be forced into flower. And they combine nicely in a vase with the white-flowering variegated dogwood. Even before there are any leaves or flowers, the fresh lime green of the *Kerria*'s branches and the brilliant deep red of the *Cornus* are a striking combination.

A
N I C E
W E E D

Greater celandine (*Chelidonium majus*) is a weed I am pleased to see in early spring. Really an old cottage herb brought to America by the colonists, it offers the very first fresh leaves in spring, other than those of the flowering bulbs. They are pretty, lettuce-green compound leaves, deeply scalloped, rising in clumps from the ground. Their fleshy, hairy stems are rather fragile and show orange sap when cut.

Greater celandine romps all over Duck Hill at the edge of the woods, by the barn, and in the garden beds where I have not weeded carefully. For several months in spring I find its greenery invaluable in bouquets as a foil for snowdrops and small daffodils and species tulips.

In April the celandine grows tall and begins to bloom, simple four-petaled flowers of clear yellow, small and star-shaped, with a mass of yellow stamens. The leaves stay green all summer (really now a gray-green) and persist after most foliage has died back in the fall. Then again I am happy to have the scalloped leaves to combine with the last Johnny-jump-ups and cottage pinks or lingering roses that I bring indoors.

❧

SPRING
RAIN

On the first warm rainy days of spring, the ducks are in heaven. If you could describe ducks as zooming (they really do waddle, after all), then that is what they are doing now, like characters in a speeded-up old movie, as they hurry from puddle to puddle, then on to the wet lawns around the gardens, jabbing their beaks into the earth in search of bugs. Always in a row, of course, and quacking softly, blissfully.

❧

CLEANUP

If the snow has melted and the ground is fairly dry by the end of March, I am in a great rush to clean up the debris in the

DUTCH CROCUSES

main garden beds, where small pools of Dutch crocuses (varieties of *C. vernus*) in lavender and purple and white are
starting to bloom. They are planted in ribbons around the
peonies and beneath the shrub roses, where they increase year
after year with no special attention — out of sight and forgotten except for this week or two when their sturdy goblets in
shining colors are the stars, the whole show, of the garden.

A small bamboo rake does a good job of clearing out the
flower borders and causes no harm as long as you rake gently
around perennials that are apt to heave with the spring thaw,
like coralbells, cottage pinks, and feverfew, and those that are
shallow-rooted, like beebalm and the various mints.

A light raking is the best way to clean up lamb's-ears
(*Stachys byzantina*), removing the tattered gray leaves and
stems to reveal the new furry green growth underneath. If the
plants still look thin and scraggly, they probably need lifting
and dividing as soon as the soil is friable; lamb's-ears benefit
from frequent division and replanting. A hard way of finding
this out is to give a few plugs of your lamb's-ears to a friend
starting a new garden, only to discover, a couple of months
later, that the friend's lamb's-ears are twice the size, incredibly
healthier and happier than any of yours.

❧

A

WHITE

CORYDALIS

As I clean up the terrace area, I am cheered to see clumps and tufts of the white fumitory (*Corydalis ochroleuca*) appearing in the cracks of the stone steps and walls and in the gravel. A gift originally from a visiting friend, this sweet little rock plant, more familiar in its common yellow form (*C. lutea*), has established itself firmly around our walled terrace. In leaf and habit it is somewhat like a tiny bleeding heart, with lacy light green foliage, glaucous beneath, that stays fresh and appealing for months. In April the corydalis starts to bloom, masses of drooping spurred white flowers touched with green and golden-yellow, and it continues to bloom untiringly right through until late autumn. The taprooted plants are difficult to move, but I am content to leave them where they seed, frothing down the steps and spreading beneath the 'Sea Foam' roses that edge the terrace. The old-fashioned lavender-blue catmint (*Nepeta mussinii*) and some Johnny-jump-ups are allowed to seed here too and are a nice accompaniment in spring to the white fumitory.

April

SIBERIAN SQUILL
(*Scilla siberica*)

By the first week of April, all sorts of garden treasures are in
bloom that would perhaps be overlooked in the lushness of
a later season. Near the kitchen door, naked jasmine and
Abeliophyllum throw off wands of starry flowers, yellow and
white. The Cornelian cherry, *Cornus mas*, standing treelike
by the barn road, is dotted all over with puffs of bright yellow,
the flowers borne in tiny umbels from the axils of older
branches. A bush of winter honeysuckle, *Lonicera fragran-
tissima*, planted outside the vegetable garden fence, quietly
opens pairs of creamy lipped flowers on stout branches, filling
the surrounding air for weeks with a soft scent of lemon.
In the herb garden, small clusters of rosy purple flowers are
out on a stiff little bush of *Daphne mezereum*. They smell
like some wonderful soap, gardenia maybe, and look pretty
blooming with the first yellow daffodils.

The early squill, *Scilla bifolia*, squat and red-stemmed,
makes a patch of soft sapphire blue under a rugosa rose in a
corner of the herb garden. Not as intense a blue as the better-
known Siberian squill (*S. siberica*), still in tight bud, the tiers

of up-facing starry flowers are nonetheless a charming bit of color.

Glory-of-the-snow (*Chionodoxa luciliae*) is flowering in sunny stretches along the woodland path. Each stem carries several starlike blooms face up, true blue fading to white at the centers. Delicately pretty up close, they are wonderfully effective when seen in masses. *C. sardensis* is similar in flower but a deeper solid blue.

Chionodoxa begins to bloom earlier than the Siberian squill, but their flowering overlaps, and they are often found together spreading under shrubs, on grassy slopes, and at the wood's edge. I will never forget the sight one early spring of a woodland walk at Dunbarton Oaks (Beatrix Farrand's masterpiece of a garden in Washington, D.C.), where glory-of-the-snow and Siberian squills had naturalized underneath the high-pruned trees, creating a dazzling carpet of blue. *C. luciliae* also comes in white and a pretty rose-pink, but they are expensive and less commonly seen.

GLORY-OF-THE-SNOW
(*Chionodoxa luciliae*)

I have a tiny sky-blue hyacinth blooming now that came here by accident a few years ago in a batch of the May-flowering *Hyacinthus amethystinus* (now called *Brimeura amethystinus*). The flower spike is just a few inches tall and is wedge-shaped, carrying bells that open from the bottom up. I believe it is called *H. azureus* or *Muscari azureum*, and it is said to thrive in a sunny sheltered spot. This little treasure needs to be seen up close (on hands and knees) to be best appreciated.

❧

DAFFODILS

Bouquets of daffodils in the house! The early trumpets and large-cupped varieties are blooming along the woodland path, and clusters of miniature daffodils open in the herb garden and flower borders — enough to justify filling a few pitchers and small jugs indoors.

The little early daffodils with characteristics of *Narcissus cyclamineus* are a special delight. 'Tête-à-Tête' is usually the first to bloom, tiny nodding trumpets of bright yellow, often two flowers to a stem, five or six inches high. This is the miniature daffodil familiar to us all, forced in pots and sold at florists and in supermarkets in February and March.

'Jack Snipe' follows on the heels of 'Tête-à-Tête'. It is slightly taller, the flower dainty and small with flared-back petals of pale yellow and a narrow bright yellow trumpet. Every year the clumps of this daffodil increase in size, offering a long-lasting, telling display of color in the border.

'February Gold', another dependable early bloomer, is similar to 'Jack Snipe' but with a bigger, jauntier flower. The petals are slightly reflexed, colored Easter yellow, the trumpet is long and narrow and gold. I have scattered this daffodil around the four back borders of the herb garden, weaving them underneath the shrub roses for a first lovely splash of color there.

'February Silver' blooms in the white garden at the same time. It is a paler, luminous version with cream petals and a yellow trumpet that fades toward white as it matures. In this half-shaded garden, it remains in flower through most of April.

The smallest trumpet daffodil of all, *Narcissus minimus*, opens its frilled trumpets in a bed of woolly thyme in the herb garden. An exact replica of the big yellow trumpets, it is just three or four inches high. The soft thyme keeps the tiny, rather squat flowers from getting splattered with mud and provides a pleasing setting of gray-green. This daffodil does not increase for me. In fact, of the dozen or so that I planted five years ago, only half that many have survived, but these give pleasure enough when they appear.

NARCISSUS 'JACK SNIPE'

ॐ

WORK
IN THE
HERB
GARDEN

As soon as the weather permits in April, I cut back hard most of the plants in the herb garden. Southernwood, lavender, thyme, sage, hyssop, winter savory, rue, and germander all benefit from a severe haircut now to keep them from getting leggy. It is a tedious job (my knees ache, my clipping hand gets sore) and time consuming, but it has its reward in the wonderful smells that are released as I handle and cut the plants.

The garden has a bare woody look when the job is done, and I am grateful for the strong pattern, the evergreen box-wood, and the fresh burgeoning foliage of other herbs like tansy and the alliums, burnet and pasqueflower, lungwort, lady's mantle, and nepeta.

Invariably some of the sages and thymes, which are marginally hardy in our harsh climate, will have died and need replacing. (I often lose golden-variegated sage and silver thyme). I have learned not to be alarmed if bushes of rue and germander look quite dead. A few weeks after they are cut back, new growth will appear from the base, and by late May the plants will be full and lush. The mints and beebalm are also slow to put forth new growth, but as I clear the beds of leaves I stir up their delicious fragrance.

Johnny-jump-ups provide some early color, seeding wildly in the beds and paths, and all sorts of small bulbs are tucked in among the herbs, creating early pools of color. By the time the

HERB GARDEN

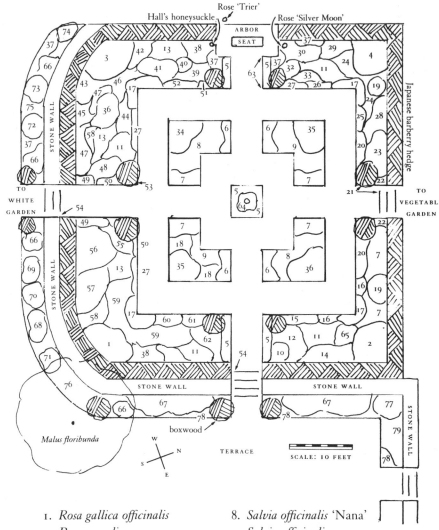

1. *Rosa gallica officinalis*
2. *Rosa mundi*
3. Rose 'Celsiana'
4. Rose 'Frau Dagmar Hartopp'
5. *Teucrium chamaedrys*
6. *Nepeta × faassenii*
7. Lavender 'Munstead' Dwarf

8. *Salvia officinalis* 'Nana'
9. *Salvia officinalis* 'Purpurescens'
10. *Salvia officinalis*
11. *Salvia superba* 'East Friesland'
12. *Achillea* 'Moonshine'

13. *Achillea* 'Coronation Gold'
14. *Iris florentina*
15. Golden lemon thyme
16. *Dianthus plumarius*
17. *Stachys byzantina*
18. *Ruta graveolens*
19. *Potentilla fruticosa* 'Katherine Dykes'
20. *Thymus vulgaris*
21. *Thymus serpyllum albus*
22. *Dianthus caesius*
23. *Allium tuberosum*
24. *Euphorbia polychroma*
25. *Santolina chamaecyparissus*
26. Silver thyme
27. *Alchemilla mollis*
28. *Agastache foeniculum*
29. *Melissa officinalis*
30. *Symphytum officinale*
31. *Convallaria majalis* 'Rosea'
32. *Anemone pulsatilla*
33. *Poterium sanguisorba*
34. *Dictamnus fraxinella*
35. *Perovskia atriplicifolia*
36. *Artemisia abrotanum*
37. *Pulmonaria saccharata*
38. *Artemisia absinthium*
39. *Mentha* × *piperita citrata*
40. *Daphne mezereum*
41. *Allium schoenoprasum*
42. *Mentha suaveolens*
43. *Digitalis purpurea*
44. *Allium cernum*
45. *Valerian officinalis*
46. *Myrrhis odorata*
47. *Monarda didyma*
48. *Mentha* × *gentilis*
49. *Allium senescens glaucum*
50. Woolly-stemmed thyme
51. *Thymus herba-barona*
52. *Oreganum vulgare* 'Aureum'
53. Woolly thyme
54. *Thymus serpyllum*
55. *Mentha suaveolens* 'Variegata'
56. *Tanacetum vulgare* 'Crispum'
57. *Sanguisorba canadensis*
58. *Salvia sclarea* var. *turkestanica*
59. *Allium senescens*
60. *Oregano onites*
61. *Thyme* × *citridorus*
62. *Salvia officinalis*, golden variegated
63. *Mentha requienii*
64. *Hedera* '238th Street'
65. *Hyssopus officinalis*
66. *Hemerocallis* varieties
67. Rose 'Sea Foam'
68. Rose 'Stanwell Perpetual'
69. Rose de Meux
70. Rose 'Petite de Holland'
71. *Daphne mezereum* 'Alba'
72. *Daphne* × *burkwoodii* 'Carol Mackie'
73. *Daphne caucasica*
74. *Hosta* 'Frances Williams'
75. *Epimedium* × *youngianum* 'Niveum'
76. *Geranium sanguineum striatum*
77. *Jasminum nudiflorum*
78. *Nepeta mussinii*
79. *Campanula persicifolia*

bulbs have finished blooming and their foliage begins to yellow, the herbs have filled out enough to hide them.

❧

LUNGWORT

AND

OTHER

DELIGHTS

Lungwort opens quietly in the early days of April. By mid-month it is in full bloom, a haze of blue, and it continues flowering right into May. It is usually the first herbaceous perennial to flower in my garden, and I treasure it for its old-fashioned charm and effectiveness as a ground cover for the early bulbs.

I have two varieties of lungwort, both indispensable. *Pulmonaria saccharata*, what I call spotted lungwort, flowers under shrubs and in shadowy nooks of the herb garden and the little white garden (where not all the flowers are white). Also known as Bethlehem sage, or spotted dog, this lungwort has clusters of soft lavender-blue bell-shaped flowers that open from pink buds. The oval leaves are rich green, spotted and splotched with what appears at a glance to be white but is actually the palest green. The leaves broaden as they mature, and even when the lungwort is not in bloom, it makes handsome clumps for the front of the border or as a ground cover. Spotted lungwort seeds around pleasantly and asks only to be shaded and watered through our brutally hot summers.

There is a white-flowering variety, *P. saccharata* 'Alba',

which I long to try and will doubtless purchase in the near future. I have as yet never bought a lungwort; mine are descendants of plants given me by a kindly neighbor when I first started gardening in earnest twenty-five years ago.

In the four angled beds of the main garden, I have encouraged *P. angustifolia* to spread under the crabapples and shrub roses. The flowers of this lungwort are a dazzling, cerulean blue, opening like spotted lungwort from pink buds. The leaves are narrower and darker in hue with no splotching. A sweep of *P. angustifolia* is stunning in its prime and serves as a complement to a succession of April's bulbs. The purple Dutch crocuses look curiously fine with the pink buds and first flowers of the lungwort. The jaunty cyclamineus daffodils are delightful companions, and later the sumptuous double daffodils rise from the lungwort's blaze of blue under the crabapples. Splashes of red and pink from the first tulips add a fillip to all the blue and white and pale yellow.

This spring we have several bluebirds visiting the main garden almost daily, and it is a thrill to see that their glorious feathers exactly echo the color of the lungwort beneath them.

Arabis (*A. caucasica* 'Snow Cap') soon follows the lungworts, its sweet-scented simple white flowers opening among felty gray-green foliage. This perennial is best among rocks where it can tumble and is pretty in combination with the blue lungworts and early scarlet tulips.

Violets begin to bloom in rich purple and rose pink and white, romping through the grass and under flowering trees at Duck Hill. I always try to take the time to pick bouquets of them for the house, but this is not a task to undertake if you are impatient or in a hurry. It means crouching on the ground (I end up sitting) while carefully slipping your fingers down

VIOLETS

the stems, nipping them one by one, until two or three dozen flowers are in hand. It is always worth the effort, for a bunch of violets surrounded by their heart-shaped leaves in a small glass vase or jug is an Edwardian delight.

Johnny-jump-ups are blooming wildly now, and their purple faces complement all the fresh clear colors of spring. They move around in my garden and come up unexpectedly in patches among the perennials and herbs. I am always happy to see them, except perhaps where they try to take over the gravel paths. Here they are pulled up easily enough, and the clumps that escape my weeder soften the hard lines of the paths.

The Siberian squill opens its drooping stars of sapphire blue around the sundial in the herb garden and spreads in drifts along the woodland path. Grape hyacinths (*Muscari botryoides*) bloom gaily at the back of the herb garden beds, a telling lavender-blue, and in one corner, pure white. These graceful spikes of bells are desirable and easy in any sunny situation where they can spread; in small bouquets with pansies and little daffodils and species tulips, they are enchanting.

I am always taken by surprise one day in April to find the woodland floor dappled with the flowers of bloodroot (*San-*

guinaria canadensis). Deeply lobed gray-green leaves suddenly unfurl to reveal white-petaled cups that open flat in the warm sun, like little single-flowered water lilies. At Duck Hill we have a treasured patch of the fragile flowers along our wooded path; at our previous home the woods were carpeted with bloodroot, and in flower, it was a thrilling sight. Bloodroot is a fleeting beauty, rarely lasting more than a day or two before its petals fall.

Almost as ephemeral, the shadblow (*Amelanchier canadensis*) opens racemes of delicate white flowers among new silver-green leaves. For a week, or longer if we're lucky, in late April, the woods around Duck Hill are starred with its ethereal blooms, for this native is a common understory tree in our area. I have planted several small shadblows along our ribbon of woods in order to enjoy the flowers up close and be able to cut a few branches to mix with daffodils for the house.

❧

THE VEGETABLE GARDEN

To a serious vegetable gardener, our vegetable garden is laughable. Only two small center beds, bounded by germander hedges, are devoted to growing vegetables. Here I have lettuces and enough tomatoes to satisfy us in summer (six plants do the job) and occasionally a row of skinny French beans or broccoli or Swiss chard. There is a clump of rhubarb in a corner of the garden and a stretch of French sorrel for soups and sauces. We have a patch of rocambole, a row of chives, some stout bushes of tarragon, a border of parsley, of course, and some chervil that has naturalized under a rose bush. Basil and dill jostle for space with the cutting flowers — zinnias, a few dahlias, Italian sunflowers, cosmos in fiery colors, and nasturtiums.

But much of this garden is given over to babies — a nursery of perennials and shrubs and occasional trees. I find a nursery area essential for growing young plants that would be engulfed and lost if placed immediately in their final destinations. Seeds of perennials started in the cold frame in March and April are transplanted here to spend their first season. Here is where I watch over rooted cuttings of shrubs and trees, mere sticks at first, until two or three years later they are large enough to be moved to their permanent places. It is satisfying (partly it's the cheap in me) to start with a twig and end up with a fine specimen of bush or tree that would cost a small fortune in a local nursery. (Quite a few enticing mail-order nurseries specialize in rooted cuttings of unusual shrubs and trees for a pittance.) This time of year I go up and down the borders checking on the young plants, pushing down any that have heaved, noting the ones that are ready to be moved, judging how much space I have for new acquisitions.

GOOSE
ON
EGGS

Gnats spin about my head as I work in the garden in the late afternoon. The horses are bedeviled by them and whinny to come in from the pasture. They shake their great heads and dance nervously by the paddock gate as we come to walk them, one by one, back to the barn.

Our pilgrim goose, Priscilla, has been sitting on a nest of eggs up at the barn for weeks. Allowing herself only a few minutes a day for food and exercise, she is faint and wobbly and losing feathers. All this for goslings we don't need — or, even worse, a heap of rotten eggs.

Miles, our gander, hisses and postures menacingly, head and neck lowered, ready to charge at anyone who approaches her. Most of the year he is a bluff and will back off if challenged, but now his warning is real, and you risk getting nipped if you venture too near.

I will be relieved when the whole episode is over and Priscilla is herself again, swimming and strutting and preening in serene, deliberate goose fashion.

❧

THUGS

As I clean up the garden borders, one of my chores is yanking out the excess of some plants that insist on spreading beyond their rightful places. Fred McGourty, in his excellent book *The Perennial Gardener*, calls such plants "thugs," and this is a fitting name. Of course, one man's garden culprits are not always another's.

Offhand, I would hardly think of violets as thugs. Sweet and delicate looking, they are high on my list of favorite flowers (the whole *Viola* family I find irresistible); but I rue the day that I ever planted the common violet in my garden beds. Innocently, I allowed some purple violets that were peppering the grass to congregate under one of the crabapples in the main garden. In another bed, under a shrub rose, I planted a dark mauvy pink violet (*V. odorata* 'Rosina') that I had ordered from a catalog. These have now multiplied and spread with a tenaciousness not to be believed, coming up through any perennials in their way.

When the violets bloom, my heart is softened, for they are a lovely sight in mass; and even when the plants are not in bloom, the heart-shaped leaves make a fine show. But I know I must dig up wads of them if they are not to take over the garden beds. I transplant them to the open woodland and place them under shrubs and flowering trees, where they make a splendid ground cover and can romp at will. In the future I will stick to the mild-mannered horned violet (*V. cornuta*) and annual Johnny-jump-ups and pansies in the flower beds.

Artemisia ludoviciana 'Silver King' is indispensable for giving pale harmony and richness to the garden. Particularly in late spring and early summer, the billowing clumps of gray-white add a soft, romantic quality to the borders. But it is an insidious creeper and will crop up all over the garden bed if not checked. So now, in April, I curb the roaming artemisia by pulling out the wayward shoots that are weaving around neighboring perennials.

When I first planted the main garden, I included the much-praised New England aster 'Harrington's Pink'. For several autumns afterward I enjoyed this late-flowering tall daisy without qualms, for it is an attractive clear pink, showy and floriferous, and I did not notice that it spread too much. Now, eight years later, the border is swamped each spring

with children of this vigorous native, some pink, some revert-
ing to the lavender-blue seen in the wild. True thugs, these
asters are deep-rooted and require some hefty digging with a
stout fork to remove. If I were to plan this garden again, I
would keep to the less rampant, lower-growing cultivars of
the New York aster, *A. novi-belgii*, for autumn color, and
plant 'Harrington's Pink' in a half-wild spot, perhaps by the
barn or among the shrubs at the edge of the woods.

At least two varieties of mint are thugs in my garden. By
the kitchen door I have an ever-burgeoning patch of spearmint (*Mentha spicata*) that I would not be without — its sprigs
are so easily gathered for summer's daily pitcher of iced tea.
Originally planted in the half-shaded bed by the doorway, the
spearmint has sneaked under an adjacent clump of hosta,
wormed beneath the edging, and marched out into the gravel
of our terrace. Every spring I yank out enough roots to fill a
bushel basket, and there is always plenty left for a season's
harvesting. What a fine refreshing fragrance this mint has.
The dark green leaves are superior for culinary uses and are
attractive as a filler in bouquets. In late summer, pale lavender
spikes of flowers are an added pleasure.

SPEARMINT
Mentha spicata

I begged a clump of ginger mint (*M.* × *gentilis* 'Variegata') from a good friend a number of years ago because I admired its yellow-variegated leaf and delicious scent. But now I dig and pull up handfuls of it yearly in a semishaded bed in the herb garden where, in my ignorance, I planted it. I know now that it is best to put the rampant mints in a place where they can flourish without hampering more delicate neighbors, yet, ideally, near enough the house to be cut and smelled.

The variegated pineapple mint (*M. suaveolens* 'Variegata'), incidentally, is not invasive, at least in my garden, and can be planted without worry among other herbs. It has a sharp, unpleasant scent to my nose, but the leaves are quite decorative, pale fuzzy green edged and splashed with white.

Apple mint (*M. rotundifolia*) romps a bit in my garden, but I let it be, and enjoy the tall stems of furry soft green leaves (so nice in a posy with old-fashioned roses) that snake through several of my half-shaded borders. In another man's garden, this mint might be considered a thug.

৺

MORE
ON
DAFFODILS

I have made a note never to plant less than twenty-five of one variety of daffodils together. Fifty or a hundred are even better if you have the room, but twenty-five of one kind make a satisfying splash in the garden beds or the woodland. Whether I follow my advice is another matter. It is so tempt-

NARCISSUS 'FLOWER RECORD'

ing with a limited purse to buy a few of this and a few of that; there are so many kinds to try.

I have an ample colony of the large-cupped narcissus 'Flower Record' under an old apple tree by the woodland path. Its rounded petals open a creamy yellow but quickly fade to crepe-paper white surrounding a shallow cup of yellow with a crimped orange edge and a green eye. This daffodil is effective when planted in quantity and increases well over the years. It is also lovely for cutting, especially when combined with the young burnished leaves of wild cherry or with white-flowered shad and bright yellow garlic mustard.

I have a weakness for double daffodils. They are opulent rather than graceful, charming in their ruffled fullness. They are particularly suited, I think, to the flower beds. 'White Lion' is a favorite. It looks like a small creamy peony and is grand in clumps under the crabapples in the main garden, where it consorts with spring phlox and lungwort and violets. Really a series of rich yellow and white ruffles, the flower has a lushness not usually associated with daffodils.

'Mary Copeland' is here, too, an appealing, fragrant, old-fashioned double, not quite as fully packed with petals as the newer varieties, white interspersed with red ruffles.

'Golden Ducat' is a fat double yellow, fuller and heavier than the old variety 'Van Sion', which is still treasured for naturalizing. I often find 'Golden Ducat' bent over after a rain, the stems not strong enough to support the weight of all those wet petals. I quickly cut the bowed heads to fill a low pitcher indoors.

The last double daffodil to bloom at Duck Hill is 'Cheerfulness'. It has fragrant clusters of creamy gardenialike flowers the size of a silver dollar on graceful stems about one and a half feet tall. 'Cheerfulness' flourishes in the center bed of the herb garden, planted around the sundial with a ground cover of ivy and bordered by a low hedge of germander. 'Yellow Cheerfulness' is identical in size and shape but is a pale butter yellow.

Blooming in the herb garden at the same time is the tiny triandus daffodil 'April Tears'. What a contrast to the double daffodils! No bigger than a snowdrop, this is a flower to see up close in the garden or to cut for small vases with violets and sprigs of herbs. Planted in a carpet of English thyme, the little reflexed flowers of soft yellow nod prettily in clusters from their slender stems.

By the end of April, the late-flowering daffodils have all opened, and their blooming period extends well into May. Pristine 'Actea' is out in drifts along the woodland path. It is perhaps the best known of the poeticus daffodils, large-flowered and fragrant, the rounded perianth snowy white, the tiny yellow cup tipped with dark red. There is an exceptional purity to its beauty.

'Pheasant's Eye' is an older poeticus, similar to 'Actea' but more delicate and smaller-flowered, with slightly recurved petals. It is ideal for naturalizing.

'Geranium', a tazetta daffodil, blooms in cheerful clusters behind the vegetable garden. It is small and sweetly fragrant, with several flowers bunched on a stem, white petaled with little orange-red cups.

'Silver Chimes' is another late-blooming tazetta, with fragrant clusters of small flowers on each stem, pure white petals surrounding tiny pale yellow cups. I have planted this enchanting daffodil around a large stone vase that sits in the center bed of the white garden. Here it blooms through a carpet of nepeta and is framed by a border of small boxwood bushes.

ð

ON PULLING WEEDS

I find I resent the visitor to my garden who stoops down to pull a weed. Yes, of course, the weed is there to be pulled — many weeds are there to be pulled — and I am sure the visitor just wants to help or show her knowledge of weeds, but for some reason I am embarrassed and find it rude. It is as if a visitor to your home paused to pick up lint from the rug or wipe a smudge from the window. I would rather not have attention drawn to the smudgy windows or the weeds in my garden. On the other hand, if a friend with time on her hands offered to come for an afternoon to help me weed, I would be ecstatic!

Every gardener has a different style of weeding. My preferred method of attack is down low, on hands and knees (a rubber kneepad is a great boon), moving slowly along the borders, scratching the soil with a three-pronged flexible weeder. I keep a clam knife in a pocket to deal with deep-rooted weeds and place a lightweight bushel basket in tossing distance to collect weeds and clippings. A trug or basket is handy for carrying scissors, clippers, and trowel, along with a pencil and pad for taking notes and some Twist-ems to tie plants up with — in fact all the paraphernalia I think I might need as I progress down the garden paths. The best and most pleasant time to weed is shortly after a rain, when the soil is loose and damp. This is a dreamlike ideal in summer, when long stretches of drought turn the soil rock-hard, and weeds, when tugged, snap off at ground level. Whenever possible, seize the moment after a blessed rain in high summer to pull those weeds and stir the soil before it again becomes dry and unyielding.

Weeding is for me the most therapeutic of gardening chores. I seem to lose myself in the smells and shapes and colors of the garden as I inch along the borders. Headaches vanish and life's problems slip away as I become immersed in this world of earth and bugs, weeds and flowers.

Ideas for garden essays often develop while I weed. My thoughts are stirred like the soil, opinions take shape as I study leaf and flower, and I stop to grab pencil and paper, sit back on the grass or retire to a shaded bench to quickly write them down while they are fresh.

May

W A T E R - L I L Y   T U L I P
(*Tulipa kaufmanniana*)

No matter how risky it is to plant tulips in the garden (it is very risky here for they are delectable to our deer), it is worth doing. No other flower adds such merriment, such a splash of color to the garden in late April and May. So I sprinkle dried blood around the emerging leaves and buds, conceal smelly soap nearby, even (in desperation) cover the opening flowers with netting at night — all (with sporadic success) to ward off the deer. One day I will succumb to the only solution and fence in the boundaries of the garden. Then I will indulge in tulipomania.

The small species tulips begin the season at Duck Hill. They are an engaging group, quite different from the hybrid Darwin and cottage and triumph tulips, smaller in height, daintier, and, for me at least, much more perennial. They tend to last for many years where they are planted, often increasing where the situation suits them. Because of their smaller size, they are best planted toward the front of borders or in the rock garden, where they can be seen up close and where they will provide radiant ribbons of color.

Tulipa kaufmanniana, the water-lily tulip, is the first to bloom, opening around the middle of April. It has rather large, lovely flowers, the shape of water lilies, that rise a few inches from broad green leaves. There are many named varieties, all of them appealing. The flowers are invariably splashed with scarlet on the outside and open to reveal cream or pale yellow at their base. I have woven water-lily tulips around the nepeta and cranesbills and hostas that edge the borders of the main garden, and here they follow the Dutch crocuses, painting strokes of merry color.

T. greigii, with handsome mottled leaves, is similar to the water-lily tulip, blooming slightly later. To me it is not as good a kind. Where *T. kaufmanniana* is graceful, *T. greigii* seems squat in comparison, and some of the salmon-colored varieties are hard to place in the garden. The color can seem harsh near yellow (forsythia is in bloom at the same time) and clear pink.

Blooming just after *T. kaufmanniana* among clumps of germander in the herb garden is the cheerful wild tulip, *T. dasystemon*. When closed, this tulip is barely noticeable, its small green buds tinged with purply brown just visible among arching straplike foliage that hugs the ground. But in the sun they open wide into pretty six-petaled stars of bright yellow and white. The flowers bloom in tight clusters only a

Tulipa dasystemon

few inches above the leaves. They do not look at all like our idea of a tulip.

T. praestans brightens the borders of our vegetable garden in late April and early May. The flowers are small, traditional in shape, and rise two or three together on eight-inch stems. Louise Beebe Wilder writes that this is her favorite red tulip, and so far in my experience I agree with her. Its "tone of scarlet is not deep but high and thin, a lovely flashing color," and it complements all the other hues of spring.

The lady tulip, or radish tulip, *T. clusiana*, is a slender species that blooms in May. Its twelve-inch stem seems tall for the size of the flower — a tiny cup of pointed petals, candy-striped red and white on the outside (one petal white, the next red). The inside of the flower is pure white with a striking purple throat. This is a dainty and exquisite tulip, charming as it rises through mats of thyme and clumps of lady's mantle in the herb garden borders. If you can bear to cut it, *T. clusiana* is enchanting in bouquets with sprigs of herbs or the red-leaved purple sand cherry (*Prunus* × *cistena*), whose tiny white flowers bloom at the same time.

T. clusiana var. *chrysantha* is similar to the lady tulip in habit and flower, growing not quite as tall, with a yellow cup streaked with red. It grows here among clumps of orange geum in a sunny border devoted to nasturtium colors — yellow and gold, orange, apricot, and scarlet.

T. batalinii ends the list of species tulips in my garden. (I long to try many others.) A sweet miniature kind, it rises from a cluster of leaves on a short stem, the flower a small plump cup of pale apricot yellow. In the herb garden the little flowers just manage to hold their heads above a patch of English thyme.

Among the tall hybrid tulips are many desirable kinds, and I never seem to have enough of them. They are not long lasting for me, partly because of the deer but also because it is their nature to fade away after a few years. This, I suppose, is why tulips are considerably less expensive than daffodils, most of which will last a lifetime.

The early single and double tulips are marvelous for beginning the hybrid tulip season. They are exceptionally long blooming, providing good splashes of color for several weeks starting here in late April. 'Bellona' is a single golden yellow variety that blooms in the four center beds of the herb garden. It is a strong yellow, a little on the garish side, but among the burgeoning greens and grays of the herbs and the clumps of dark purple, yellow-faced Johnny-jump-ups, the eye is not offended by its strong color. By the time these tulips are over in late May, the herbs have leafed out fully and nicely hide the fading tulip foliage.

I grow two of the early double tulips, 'Murillo Max' and 'Peach Blossom', both pink and charming and un-tuliplike. They look more like tiny peonies, nodding with the weight of their petals, and they are sweet planted among early-blooming perennials or cut for mixed bouquets.

For late May color I plant the tall-growing Darwin and cottage tulips in shades of pink in the main garden. 'Clara Butt' and 'Queen of Bartigons', 'Princess Elizabeth' and the striped 'Sorbet' provide a few years of rosy color (deer willing) before they fade away.

The lily-flowered tulip 'White Triumphator' is woven through the two long beds of the white garden. It is a tall, elegant tulip with deep cups of pointed petals that gently reflex as they age. It makes a lovely late-May picture in this small shadowy garden with bushes of boxwood and lavender catmint (*Nepeta × faassenii*), white coralbells, and violas. In the background a native dogwood tree is in full bloom, its graceful sweeping branches littered with snowy white bracts.

One variety of tulips introduced in the 1950s that the catalogs tout is called giant Darwin hybrids. I have tried them and confess I don't like them. Giant they are, with huge flowers in the gaudiest colors. The gaudy colors can look fine in the right place, but it is only after a few years, when the size of their flowers diminishes, that the giant Darwins start to look attractive in the garden. As so often happens, the hybridizers, intent on producing the biggest and most brilliant flower, have sacrificed all its grace.

I have finally this fall planted some parrot tulips in the vegetable garden for cutting. Who can look at the flower paintings of the old Dutch masters without craving these fantastic striated and feathered flowers for mixed bouquets indoors?

AN
EPIMEDIUM

I was given an epimedium two years ago by a gardening neighbor, and I am eager to write of its charm. It is a white-flowering variety called *Epimedium × youngianum* 'Niveum' and I cannot imagine a more delicately pretty plant. It is in flower now, tiny sprays of drooping bells suspended above arrow-shaped light green leaves slightly tinged with bronze.

It grows in soft low mounds and makes a delightful ground cover under a bush of *Daphne* × *burkwoodii* in a half-shaded spot near the white garden. The dainty flowers can be cut for small nosegays, mixing nicely with the little daffodils or wild tulips and catmint and Johnny-jump-ups.

The epimediums are said to prefer a deep, humus-rich soil and will even grow in full shade. The clumps increase slowly and can be extended by division in early spring. The leaves remain attractive all summer and fall and therefore make a first-rate ground cover beneath shrubs and deciduous trees. There are varieties with rose-pink, yellow, and red flowers as well as white.

❧

LILACS

I associate lilacs with Duck Hill. They were here when we came, when there was no garden at all — great clumps of the common lilac, thick-trunked, bent with age, but nonetheless laden with flowers in early May. How appropriate those purple buds and lavender trusses seemed against the pale yellow of the farmhouse and how splendidly they filled the air with their fragrance. I have left them as they were, merely trimming out some suckers and dead wood, and in early spring enriching the soil around them with manure from the barnyard and wood ashes from the fireplaces. And I have planted several other kinds of lilacs to extend their season.

Although the common lilac (*Syringa vulgaris*) and some of its many varieties are unsurpassed for opulence of flower and fragrance, there are a number of other excellent species and hybrids. Some are smaller in size and more graceful in habit, making them especially suitable to our smaller gardens. Many of them, too, are not beset with the mildew that disfigures the leaves of the common lilac.

The Rouen lilac (*S.* × *chinensis*) blooms just as the common lilac is fading. It is an arching shrub with an airy, delicate look, in leaf and in size slightly smaller than the common lilac from which it descends. The myriad flowers on my bush are purple and sweet smelling, held in loose trusses that are ideal for bouquets.

The Persian lilac, (*S.* × *persica*), which is the Rouen lilac's other parent, is smaller still (about five or six feet in height) with the same delicate habit and a light fragrance. It blooms lavishly in mid-May. Russell Page recommends planting "five young plants together" for the best effect and notes that "they are particularly lovely hanging over a low wall or on the bank above a pool, reflected in the water." I have planted a clump of lavender ones with some old-fashioned yellow shrub roses behind the vegetable garden fence.

In late May the daphne lilac (*S. microphylla* 'Superba')

DAPHNE LILAC
(*Syringa microphylla* 'Superba')

opens slender plumes of pale pink flowers from soft garnet buds. The flowers are intensely fragrant and are marvelous to smell outdoors, but in the confines of a small room, their sweetness is cloying. This is a stunning lilac, rather different in flower and habit from its relatives. The bush has a lax, broad shape, growing about six feet high and twice as wide, and consequently is ideal to clothe a sunny bank. The daphne lilac has the odd custom of reblooming in August. Garden visitors unfamiliar with this lilac, seeing my clumps in delicate bloom at the end of the summer, have wondered what mysterious and wonderful shrub it is.

The dwarf Korean lilac (*S. meyeri* 'Palibin') blooms in my garden at the end of May. It is a small, compact lilac (my bushes are about four feet high and wide), rounded in shape, with tiny dark green leaves. It is literally covered with pale pinkish mauve flowers that open from deeper mauve buds. This is a perfect lilac to include in the perennial garden, for it looks completely at home in the company of iris and lemon daylilies and a carpet of cranesbills. It is strongly, pleasantly fragrant.

The last lilac to bloom at Duck Hill, as the dwarf Korean lilac fades, is *S. patula* 'Miss Kim'. It is another low-growing kind but looser, more vase-shaped in habit and with larger leaves. The dusty mauve buds open into palest lavender flowers that fade to skim-milk white. This is an elegant lilac in flower. Its one drawback is the lack of strong lilac fragrance. Here it is planted at a corner of the house by the terrace, where it is a fine picture in bloom with yellow-green lady's mantle foaming beneath it.

Some lilacs do not bloom when very young, and we must wait with the utmost patience for several years after planting before being rewarded with their panicles of flowers. The daphne lilac and dwarf Korean lilac are exceptions to this rule, often blooming the season after they are planted.

CHICKENS
IN THE
GARDEN

There are two weeds in my garden that the chickens relish. One is the persistent chickweed (aptly named), the other a little annual plant called carpetweed. Both are low-growing stringy plants that creep among the perennials. It is comical to watch the chickens eat them for they draw the long stringy bits of weeds into their beaks like strands of spaghetti.

I wonder, idly, if I manage to rid my garden of these weeds, whether the chickens would feast on a treasured perennial instead. But the likelihood of a weedless garden is faint, and the chickens do little damage as they parade around on their afternoon tour of the borders.

The small vegetable garden, however, is very much off limits. The barberry hedge and a fence fashioned of rustic wood and chicken wire help to keep them out, but once in a while they discover they can hop up the stone steps into the herb garden and on into the vegetable garden and must be quickly shooed away. Chickens will devour lettuce seedlings in seconds, and their scratching for bugs can instantly ruin carefully sown rows of lettuces and beans and cutting flowers.

#

DUCK

HILL

CRABAPPLES

In the past nine years, we have planted three kinds of crab-apple trees near the house. The great old sugar maples that originally shaded our farmhouse were felled by storms and old age before we arrived. Reveling in the sunshine that flooded in the windows and would allow roses and herbs and perennials to flourish just outside, I was not tempted to re-place those maples. But the house sat starkly on its small hill; we needed some kind of tree to cast a light shade and give vertical interest to the scene.

Standard apple trees would have been an appropriate choice because our village was a cider-mill town in the nine-teenth century, and apple trees are still in evidence every-where. Three commercial orchards remain, supplying the neighborhood with cider and apples every fall; but the land is becoming too valuable, greedy developers are closing in, and soon there will be houses among those rows of apple trees. As you walk in the woods around the village, it is common to find ancient gnarled apples among the maples and ash and hickories. Even at Duck Hill we have one grand old apple tree alongside the woodland path.

Although there is nothing lovelier, I think, than apple blossoms, nor more pleasant than a meadow with high grass and rows of apple trees underplanted with daffodils in spring, crabapples are a more practical choice for the small garden. Apple trees require pruning to keep them in shape (and some would say spraying), and in autumn the falling fruit must be coped with. Ornamental crabapples, on the other hand, need little or no pruning, for they grow naturally in picturesque shapes. Their fruits are small and decorative, persisting on the trees well into winter, when they are eventually eaten by the birds.

We chose the 'Katherine' crabapple to mark the four corners of the main garden. It is a charming small tree that grows loosely upright to about fifteen or twenty feet, then spreads gracefully outward. In early May it is a pink and white confection, covered with masses of pink buds that open to pale pink double flowers and fade to white. In autumn it is hung all over with small golden fruits blushed with red.

At a corner of the terrace, we planted a Japanese flowering crabapple (*Malus floribunda*) to provide shade for our alfresco summer lunches. This old-time crabapple was introduced to this country in the 1860s and is still considered one of the best. It is densely branched and rounded in form, with a picturesque sweeping growth to twenty or thirty feet. The flowers are small and single, dark pink (almost red) in bud gradually fading to white. They do not all open at once, so the tree at flowering time is prettily speckled with rose-red and pink and white. The small fruits hanging in clusters are flushed with yellow and red in the fall and are savored by the songbirds.

This spring we have planted four trees of a fairly new variety of crabapple called 'Snowdrift' in our new courtyard. 'Snowdrift' is a denser, more upright-growing tree than 'Katherine' and not as large as the Japanese crab. It has glossy dark green leaves and masses of large single white flowers that open from red buds. The fruit, also red, persists on the branches through much of the winter.

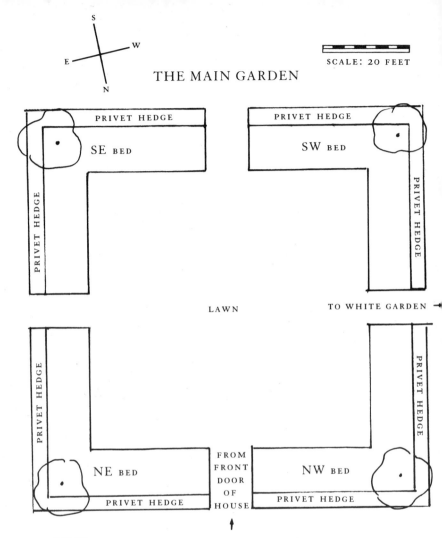

THE MAIN GARDEN

SCALE: 20 FEET

S W E N

PRIVET HEDGE

SE BED

PRIVET HEDGE

PRIVET HEDGE

SW BED

PRIVET HEDGE

LAWN

TO WHITE GARDEN →

PRIVET HEDGE

NE BED

PRIVET HEDGE

PRIVET HEDGE

NW BED

PRIVET HEDGE

FROM FRONT DOOR OF HOUSE

NOTE:

The south beds are partially shaded by high maples to the south along our boundary. They get morning and late afternoon sun.

The north beds are in full sun.

There is a Katherine crabapple in each corner.

A succession of spring-flowering bulbs and lilies are interwoven among the perennials and shrubs.

❧

T W O

D A P H N E S

Two excellent varieties of daphne are blooming now in a partially shaded bed beneath the herb garden wall. Both are splendidly suitable for the small garden, growing in compact rounded bushes to three or four feet. They are densely covered with glossy foliage that remains attractive through the entire growing season and lingers on the bushes into winter. Best of all, for many weeks they are spangled with deliciously fragrant flowers.

Daphne × *burkwoodii* 'Carol Mackie' is a handsome shrub with variegated leaves that grow in whorls, rather like the leaves of a euphorbia, and are deep green edged in creamy yellow. It is such an attractive bush in leaf that I wouldn't mind if it didn't bloom. But it does, for most of May, with clusters of small pale pink flowers that release a heavenly fragrance. For those who do not like variegated leaves, other selections of this hybrid daphne have solid green foliage.

The other bush beneath the herb garden wall is *D. caucasica*, one of the species daphnes from which *D.* × *burkwoodii* was developed. It has the same superb habit, the same narrow leaves, glossy and dark green. The flowers are similar in shape, tiny four-lobed stars in terminal clusters that open from mauvy pink buds and fade to white. It, too, is intensely fragrant in flower. But this daphne goes a step further. It blooms heavily in May, rests a bit, then starts to flower again in summer and continues right through October. I cannot think of another shrub in my garden that blooms this long.

Daphnes have the bad reputation of being finicky. For no

apparent reason, they are apt to die suddenly. At best they are considered short-lived. But these two daphnes, at least, are so superlative in habit and in flower that they are worth the gamble to have in the garden.

DOGWOODS

Cornus florida

It has been a great sorrow to watch the decline of our native dogwood tree, *Cornus florida*. Some years ago a fungus disease began to spread among our dogwoods on the East Coast and now, where the roadsides and woodlands were renowned for their blizzard of white and pink flowers in May, only a spattering of dogwood blossoms remains.

But as I walk through the fields and woods surrounding Duck Hill, I see many young saplings of dogwood coming along that seem healthy. Maybe in another decade this most glorious of our native trees will be abundant again.

Plantsmen are advising us to grow the Japanese dogwood (*C. kousa*) instead. This is a handsome tree, growing upright and then spreading out as it ages, with masses of white stars (flower bracts) in June. Decorative raspberrylike fruits follow the flowers, and in the fall the leaves turn gorgeous colors of scarlet and copper. The trunks of mature kousa dogwoods become beautifully mottled with tan and pale gray.

But the Japanese dogwood does not resemble *C. florida* in habit, and to me it is not a completely satisfying substitute. Our native dogwood is a very light, delicate tree with a horizontal form of growth. It is perfect for filtering through woodland and growing beneath larger trees at the edge of meadows or lawns, where its snowy branches sweep the ground. The kousa dogwood, on the other hand, is bushier, stouter in feeling, denser, and more upright without the same grace. Only in old age does it take on a horizontal look with spreading branches. Even its flowering has a heavier look; it is spectacular in bloom rather than delicate and natural, more appropriate as a specimen tree than as a woodland underplanting.

The doublefile viburnum (*V. plicatum* var. *tomentosum*) blooms at the same time as our native dogwood and has a similar feeling, with disks of white flowers on gracefully sweeping horizontal branches. Several bushes of these planted in a wave at the edge of the lawn are a possible substitute for our ailing dogwoods.

KOUSA DOGWOOD
(*Cornus kousa*)

JOHNNY-JUMP-UPS

Gertrude Jekyll advises us not to spot flowers in the garden "like buttons on a waistcoat," and I know from experience that her advice is wise. One sweep of pale yellow daylilies, for instance, is more effective than single clumps spotted along the border. This is a hard lesson to learn. I am always tempted to spread the wealth by sprinkling a good plant here and there in the garden.

On the other hand, I do think there are some exceptions to Miss Jekyll's rule. It is nice sometimes to repeat a pool of color farther along in the border. And certain plants, like peonies, *Dictamnus*, *Baptisia australis*, and shrub roses, have enough bulk that they can be effectively used as single specimens in the flower border, woven together by drifts of other complementary flowers around them. Furthermore, it is always visually pleasing to emphasize an axis or a path by repeating certain plants at intervals along its length. Not flowers necessarily, but plants that catch the eye because of their color or shape — gray lamb's-ears, for instance, or round bushes of box, decorative pots of geraniums, roses shaped into standards, pyramids of yew, or flowering fruit trees.

Those exceptions aside, there is no question that large drifts and pools of one flower are always satisfying to the eye.

Rarely is this done on a more lavish scale than in nature, where acres of fields are lit with goldenrod or a pink haze of ragged robin, or washed with ice-blue chicory; and the roadsides for miles are ablaze with magenta loosestrife or dusted white with Queen Anne's lace.

Perhaps this is why old gardens are often more visually pleasing than new ones. The gardener has calmed down, resigned himself to growing the plants that particularly flourish for him; over the years, these have been endlessly lifted and divided and replanted, and have resulted in large handsome drifts.

A garden nearby is a good example of this. It has been owned and cared for by the same woman, now in her nineties, since she was first married some seventy years ago. It is a lovely garden, very simple now, with bold drifts of a few plants for each season. I was last there in July, when the borders were aglow with vast stretches of a clear yellow daylily (the old 'Hyperion' perhaps) and a deeper yellow yarrow. White peachbells and feverfew wove in and out near the front of the border where fat ribbons of lamb's-ears edged the waving beds. In the background one grand clump of ruby-red hollyhocks gave a vertical accent and, with an old crimson climbing rose, brought depth of color to the picture.

Certain good plants tend to seed about, and if we are not too tidy or ruthless with the weeder and allow them their way, they can bring an unforeseen harmony to the garden. Foxgloves do this at Duck Hill, seeding all around the rich borders, often growing with an extravagance (in numbers) and boldness (in situation) that I would not have dared. They bring magic to the garden in early June and are a perfect complement to the peonies and iris and old shrub roses.

A little pink woodland forget-me-not (*Myosotis sylvatica*) spreads beneath the shrub roses in one of the damper beds of the garden and sows itself around the lungwort and hostas and early double tulips, creating unexpected pictures that often delight me. Johnny-jump-ups, of course, are a recurring theme in my garden, often coloring the ground with deep purple among the perennials and herbs. When they begin to get leggy in midsummer, I pull the plants up and discard them, knowing that next spring there will be new drifts of this endearing viola.

The tall white-flowering annual nicotiana, prized for its nighttime fragrance, threads itself (from seed) through my half-shaded borders. Our native blue lobelia (*L. siphilitica*) is another welcome self-seeder, adding a haze of soft blue spikes to the garden in August and September. Not surprisingly, it is often with nature's helping hand that we achieve those drifts of flowers that paint the prettiest pictures in our gardens.

❧

A
DELUGE
OF
RAIN

The ducks have discovered a trench I had dug for more hemlock hedging. It is about fifty feet long and two feet wide and deep. A steady downpour has filled the trench with water, and all day long the ducks have been swimming up and down it as though it were their own private canal.

We have had eleven inches of rain so far this month —

thunderous, drenching rain. Flower buds rot, black spot and mildew begin their stealthy advance, and weeds leap up in the gravel paths and flower beds as soon as I turn my back.

I feel overwhelmed by the struggle against the elements of nature. The caterpillars are back after an eight-year hiatus, all sizes and colors of them. They make brown lacework of the roses' foliage and eat lustily in the crabapples, leaving holes and droppings in their wake. A quick-hopping beetle is disfiguring my astilbe and lady's mantle and clumps of spearmint by the kitchen door. Last night deer got into the garden and dined on hosta and summer phlox. The Japanese beetles are still to come.

There is no moderation in our weather, only excesses. Every year we are faced with pests and diseases. And yet, through it all we doggedly persevere, knowing that we will have our reward in a fragrant blossom or an occasional pretty stretch of garden.

In the rain today I gathered a handful of sweetly scented lilies of the valley for a small glass vase on my bureau. Surely it is one of the treats of May that makes the struggle worthwhile.

BUTTERCUPS

I think I have never noticed before how very brilliant the yellow of buttercups is. It is not a golden yellow, not the color of school buses and road signs, but rather an intense pure yellow, squeezed straight from the tube undiluted, with a high gloss, like the color of children's rain slickers.

It is a yellow so bright that if Nature had painted it in big

BUTTERCUPS

strokes it would be blinding. But buttercups are small (the rounded petals encircling the green boss make up a flower about the size of a penny) and are usually seen scattered in a meadow, not growing thickly in masses. They are mere dots of shimmering brilliance in a field of soft green.

꙰

A

LULL

For about a week near the end of May, there is a lull in the garden. The splashy tulips are fading, and the great buxom peonies have yet to open. But many quieter flowers are blooming now among the fresh burgeoning greens and grays of the garden.

Old-fashioned bleeding hearts (*Dicentra spectabilis*) are dripping with candy hearts in the half-shaded borders. The fringed bleeding hearts (*D. eximia*) are covered with more modest flowers in rose-pink and white, and will continue to bloom tirelessly all summer above mounds of lacy foliage. Unlike their more spectacularly flowering relative, which goes dormant halfway through summer, these bleeding hearts are excellent front border plants for beds that are not too dry or sunny.

Thalictrum aquilegifolium, the columbine meadow rue, opens soft puffs of mauvy purple flowers next to a clump of early-blooming lavender iris. Bright orange geum, with its pretty roselike flowers, dances toward the front of the nasturtium border near some peach-pink dwarf iris. Lady's mantle froths with tiny chartreuse flowers above mounds of pleated dew-filled leaves in the herb garden.

Nepeta × *faassenii*, the best of the catmints, opens sprays of lavender blue above gray-green foliage. This is one of the most effective plants to use as a front edging in a perennial border or with roses, and there are few sunny garden beds where I do not have stretches of it. It blooms for a long time

FRINGED BLEEDING HEART
(*Dicentra eximia*)

(late May and June and into July), then rests and reblooms in August and September. The foliage is lovely in the spring, forming clumps of soft, telling gray-green, and if sheared in midsummer, it renews itself and remains attractive into fall.

In lightly shaded borders, sweet cicely (*Myrrhis odorata*) opens delicate wheels of white flowers above beautiful ferny foliage that smells of licorice when rubbed. Columbines that have seeded themselves bloom shyly here among the hostas and astilbes. The pretty lavender spring phlox (*P. divaricata*), which sends waves of fragrance into the air, blooms in shadowy places under the crabapples with woodland forget-me-nots.

The beautybush (*Kolkwitzia amabilis*) drips branches of tubular pink flowers above the herb garden, and small bushes of *Deutzia gracilis*, smothered in white flowers, border the vegetable garden fence.

Then, suddenly, the early roses start to bloom and give us a preview of the wealth of flowers and fragrance to come in June.

ॐ

MAY

ROSES

The month-long pageant of old shrub roses begins here quietly around the end of May. *Rosa glauca* (formerly called *R. rubrifolia*) is usually the first to bloom. It has charming small single flowers of a bright clear pink with white centers, borne in clusters on the rose's arching branches. But *R. glauca* is better known for its foliage. Its leaves and young stems are extraordinarily attractive, usually described as plum-colored, but really a blend of grayish green and purple, tinged with copper. The foliage is much prized by flower arrangers, and for the same reason it makes an excellent foil in the flower garden. This rose is best planted toward the back of the border, for it rises to six or seven feet before gracefully arching over. *R. glauca* blooms prettily for several weeks, then neatly drops its flower petals. By summer, hips have developed, at first a greenish beige, turning in autumn a nice dusky red.

Many of the old-fashioned yellow roses begin to bloom now. The fern-leaved 'Father Hugo' (*R. hugonis*) opens sprays of butter-yellow single flowers on good-sized bushes of prickly reddish stems. 'Father Hugo' grows here in the grass behind the vegetable garden with some bushes of honeysuckle and lilacs. It is said not to like coddling and is very hardy.

Its sport, *R. cantabrigiensis*, I do pamper a bit, however. This is a heavenly rose, slender and tall, with prickly, loosely arching branches and ferny foliage similar to that of 'Father

Rosa glauca

Rosa cantabrigiensis

Hugo'. The flowers are similar too, but are larger and a paler yellow, luminous really, the color of unsalted butter. They have a light sweet fragrance. *R. cantabrigiensis* grows in a sunny bed in the main garden among *Artemisia* 'Silver King' and clumps of a soft yellow iris and lavender nepeta.

'Agnes' is a luscious yellow rugosa rose. I fell in love with it a few years ago at the New York Botanical Garden, where huge bushes are covered in May with soft yellow double flowers. It has a strong delicious fragrance and the typical marvelous rugosa foliage — crinkled and deep green. Two bushes of 'Agnes' are now planted at Duck Hill, one among violets and bleeding hearts in the main garden, the other mingling with white single peonies and orange geums in the nasturtium border.

Two other rugosas are in full bloom and fill the air with their scent. 'Blanc Double de Coubert' is planted in opposite corners of the white garden. It has papery, chalk-white flowers that are loosely double, opening from long, elegant buds. The flowers are particularly handsome against the glossy dark green ribbed leaves. After the first flush of bloom, you can expect an occasional flower through September. The rugged foliage remains good-looking all summer and turns an attractive soft yellow in October.

In the herb garden, surrounded by the chartreuse flowers of the cushion euphorbia (*E. epithymoides*) and gray lamb's-ears, 'Frau Dagmar Hartopp' opens large simple flowers of silvery pink. This is a small-growing rugosa, about three feet high and wide, and it blooms off and on throughout the summer. If I haven't deadheaded all the flowers, 'Frau Dagmar Hartopp' is covered in autumn with wonderful hips, the size and color of cherry tomatoes. This, and all the rugosas, have the almost unique asset among roses of disease-free foliage. Even the persistent Japanese beetles find their glossy leaves unpalatable.

I love to bury my nose in the first early blooms of the hybrid burnet rose 'Stanwell Perpetual'. This is the first rose of the season that has, for me, the true intoxicating old rose scent. It is a four-foot arching shrub, very prickly, with small ferny leaves and rumpled blooms of palest pink. Gertrude Jekyll, in *Roses for English Gardens*, recommends planting it in clumps of three, but my one bush looks graceful enough against the low herb garden wall, where it is underplanted with mounds of pale pink *Geranium sanguineum* var. *striatum*. By the beginning of June this rose is a fountain of bloom, and it continues to flower lightly until frost.

June

PEONY 'SARAH BERNHARDT'

Is any major garden flower more fleeting than the peony? If we are lucky, if there are no thundering storms, no wind or pelting rain, the great voluptuous blooms will last in flower a week before dropping their wads of silky petals on the ground. We can extend their period of bloom by planting early- and late-flowering kinds (most catalogs will tell you which they are); nonetheless, their extravagant show is short-lived.

Unless you have a lot of garden space, it is best, therefore, "not to go hog wild" with peonies, as Henry Mitchell puts it in his delightful book *The Essential Earthman*. Planting a few varieties among perennials and shrubs in a mixed border seems to me the best way to use them. In the beginning of June they herald the season of extravagant bloom, and through the summer and fall their handsome leaves remain a good foil for other flowers woven around them.

I have some unnamed Edwardian peonies that I brought from my old garden, where they had outlasted several generations of owners, and among my collection of double-flowering kinds they are favorites. The flowers, blush pink fading to white, clear pink, or pure white with buttery centers, are smaller than the ones I have since bought, earlier blooming, and have the best fragrance, an odd roselike sweetness.

The giant-flowered peonies that are sold in catalogs I sometimes think look better in bouquets than they do in the garden. On the dining room table right now is a large blue-and-white jar full of blush-pink double blooms as big as luncheon plates (a variety called 'Nick Shaylor'), mixed with branches of flowering mock orange, fernleaf tansy, and the nubby pink flower stalks of French sorrel. It is a show-stopping bouquet. But in the garden these flowers seem overscaled, almost gross in their largeness, and not in harmony with the small, exquisite flowers of the old-fashioned shrub roses opening around them.

All the double peonies require staking to hold up their heavy blooms, and this is best done by sinking three or four thin bamboo stakes around each plant, then circling the stakes with flexible plastic green ribbon or twine. I do this in mid- to late May, before the peonies flower, when it is fairly easy to conceal the stakes and ribbon with peony foliage. One great lady called 'Sarah Bernhardt' is so full of huge, luscious pink petals that she leans over anyway and rests her voluminous flowers on the great ribbed blue-green leaves of *Hosta sieboldiana* 'Elegans' growing beneath her. This is a picture that always pleases — the color combination is splendid, and the two plants complement each other in scale.

The single-flowered and Japanese varieties of peonies last longer for me in flower, perhaps because their blooms are not so heavy with petals and can better withstand the rain and

JAPANESE-STYLE PEONY

wind. Happily, many of these are not huge in scale. 'Krinkled White' is a lovely single of modest size with ruffled white petals surrounding a cluster of yellow stamens. 'Sea Shell' has a delicate cup of large satiny pink petals around golden stamens. 'Scarlet O'Hara' is a stunning early-blooming single that is not scarlet but a rich crimson fading to rose pink. (I ordered this peony from a catalog to plant in the nasturtium border, thinking it would be a bright, almost fire-engine, red. But I should know better. So few flowers that are billed as "scarlet" in catalogs actually turn out to be that color.)

Peonies provide delightful opportunities for companion plantings of bulbs. Dutch crocuses and the early small daffodils can be tucked in closely around them to bloom with the emerging reddish buds. Tulips planted nearby are enhanced by the peonies' young foliage, which is often a handsome mahogany-tinged green. Summer- and fall-blooming lilies look marvelous planted among clumps of peonies, for the tall stalks of the lilies are softened by the peony foliage through which they rise and bloom.

Peonies, once planted, take little care. They have no need to be divided and will continue blooming tirelessly in one spot for decades. On the other hand, if you do have to move them, they are obliging, skipping one season of bloom at most. They like a rich soil with some lime mixed in if the soil is very acid, and prefer a sunny position. If peonies are planted too deeply, it is said they will fail to flower; plant the crowns with their red buds just an inch or two below the soil line.

OLD
SHRUB
ROSES

DAMASK ROSE 'MADAME HARDY'

For a brief and glorious three weeks in June, I am not mumbling excuses about the state of my garden. It is "the time of perfect young summer," Gertrude Jekyll writes in *Wood and Garden*, "the fulfillment of the promise of the earlier months, and with as yet no sign to remind one that its fresh young beauty will ever fade." Paths and flower beds are weeded, edges are trim, the lawn is a velvety green, and there is an extravagance of flower and fragrance that will not be equaled the rest of the growing season.

Fountains of old-time roses are in bloom — damasks, albas, centifolias, and gallicas — filling the air with their sweetness. These are the roses that seem most at home in the mixed flower borders, tumbling about groups of iris and foxgloves, peonies and campanulas, underplanted with catmint, pinks, and cranesbills. They have a gracefulness and a romantic look unmatched by modern roses, their smaller flowers produced in lavish profusion, their fragrance rich and thrilling.

Among the old shrub roses, the albas are my favorites. They make lovely bushes, about five feet high and wide, with arching branches of blue-green foliage. Their flowers encompass the most beautiful tints of white to pink and have a pure, delicious scent. Like most of the old roses, the albas have only this one stretch of flowering, but if our weather is not too humid (causing black spot) and the Japanese beetles not too voracious, their attractive leaves are a pleasing background all summer.

'Celeste' (or 'Celestial') is an enchanting alba with pale pink flowers somewhere between single and double. Planted here in one of the half-shaded borders of the main garden, bushes of 'Celeste' consort with blue and white peachbells (*Campanula persicifolia*), purple Siberian iris, and soft pink *Geranium macrorrhizum*. 'Maiden's Blush' is another five-foot alba beauty with exquisite blush-pink double flowers massed on graceful branches among blue-green leaves. It has been a favorite cottage flower here and in England for centuries. In his classic book on old roses, Graham Stuart Thomas says, "To me there is no rose scent so pure and refreshingly delicious as that of the Maiden's Blush." 'Queen of Denmark' ('Königin von Dänemark') is a similar alba but with deeper pink flowers that remind me of swirled strawberry ice cream. It jostles for space in the garden between the dwarf Korean lilac and bushes of *Baptisia*, and is underplanted with clumps of rue and coralbells. 'Felicité Parmentier' is a narrower alba

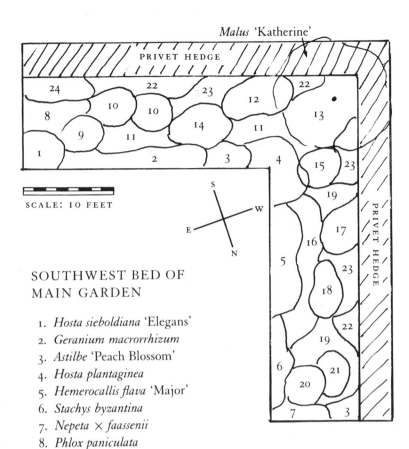

Malus 'Katherine'

PRIVET HEDGE

PRIVET HEDGE

SCALE: 10 FEET

S
W
E
N

SOUTHWEST BED OF MAIN GARDEN

1. *Hosta sieboldiana* 'Elegans'
2. *Geranium macrorrhizum*
3. *Astilbe* 'Peach Blossom'
4. *Hosta plantaginea*
5. *Hemerocallis flava* 'Major'
6. *Stachys byzantina*
7. *Nepeta* × *faassenii*
8. *Phlox paniculata*
9. Peony 'Sarah Bernhardt'
10. Rose 'Celeste'
11. *Hemerocallis* 'Hyperion'
12. *Astilbe* 'Professor van der Weilen'
13. *Phlox divaricata*
14. Siberian iris, lavender blue
15. Rose 'Charles de Mills'
16. *Monarda* 'Croftway Pink'
17. *Rosa glauca*
18. Rose 'New Dawn'
19. *Aster novae-angliae* 'Alma Potschke'
20. *Rosa gallica officinalis*
21. Rose 'Striped Moss'
22. *Digitalis purpurea*
23. *Tanacetum vulgare* 'Crispum'
24. *Astilbe taquetii* 'Superba'

NOTE:
Roses underplanted with *Pulmonaria angustifolia*.
Pink forget-me-nots seed under privet hedge.

with smaller swirled blooms of the palest pink, fading to white. Here, in a sunny border, it mingles with spotted foxgloves and the milky blue bells of *Campanula lactiflora*.

The globular blooms of the centifolia, or "cabbage" rose, are familiar to us in Dutch and French floral art of past centuries. It was a common plant in Gertrude Jekyll's day; she wrote, "No rose surpasses it in excellence of scent; it stands alone as the sweetest of all its kind, as the type of the true rose smell." 'Fantin Latour' is a tall arching centifolia, remarkably thornless, that becomes a fountain of romantic blooms. The drooping flowers are packed with medium to pale pink petals and are richly fragrant. Growing in a rather lax and open way, and measuring five feet by five feet, it is a good rose for the corner of a garden bed. After years of lavish bloom, 'Fantin Latour' is dying out in a corner of the main garden, perhaps because of a recent brutal drought. I would not like to be without this rose and will certainly plant it again.

The rose 'Common Moss' (*R. centifolia* 'Muscosa') is a sport of the centifolia beloved by the Victorians. It is a tall, gaunt shrub with blooms that are similar to 'Fantin Latour' in color, fragrance, and shape, but with fuzzy or mossy sepals that enfold its buds and frame its flowers. A posy of moss roses with some sprigs of southernwood and apple mint is a memorable treat. Three other centifolias grow in my garden. 'Petite de Holland' is a small shrub (three feet) with charming miniature cabbage blooms that are clear pink and sweetly fragrant. 'Rose de Meux', equally small and scented, has tiny pink pom-pom blooms. Dean Hole, the Victorian rosarian, calls them "the pony roses" of his childhood. The lovely buds are valued for potpourri. The third rose, 'Striped Moss', is a rather wayward shrub with small appealing flowers that are striped crimson and pale pink, framed with the telltale mossy sepals.

The ancient damask roses, softly colored and intensely fragrant, have always been cherished as a source for attar of roses, rose water, and potpourri. Perhaps the most famous damask today is the beautiful 'Madame Hardy'. It is a stout five-foot bush covered with small white double blooms that open flat, swirled and quartered around a curious green button eye. The flowers are unique and sumptuous in the garden and in bouquets. The foliage is bright green and, alas, appealing to Japanese beetles; later in the season it often looks ratty. I mask this with Michaelmas daisies, summer phlox, and the late-blooming hosta 'Honeybells'. Earlier, magenta-pink *Geranium sanguineum* and cheerful yellow evening primroses complement the white roses. 'Celsiana', a lovely damask blooming in the herb garden, has feminine, ruffled pink flowers on a slight, arching four-foot shrub with downy light green leaves. Its fragrance is exquisite. The venerable 'Autumn Damask' ('Quatre Saisons', *R. damascena bifera*), which repeats its flowering into October, is one of the most fragrant of all. Although the bush is somewhat scraggly, I prize the sweet, loosely double flowers of clear pink and collect them carefully in a basket to dry for potpourri.

Similar in shape and scent to the damasks, the nineteenth-century portland roses delight us with a second flush of flowering in late summer that is equal to, if not lovelier than, their first. 'Comte de Chambord' makes a neat four-foot by three-foot shrub at the entrance to the main garden. It has rich pink double flowers, deeply scented, that are born singly and are closely framed with large green leaves. Graham Stuart Thomas describes this portland characteristic as the "high-shouldered" look. Smaller in stature, with flowers a lighter pink, 'Jacques Cartier' is another portland beauty with a heady fragrance. Two bushes of this rose stand across from 'Comte de Chambord', underplanted with lady's mantle and interwoven with regal lilies.

The gallicas are the oldest of all the shrub roses and encompass some of the liveliest colors. They tend to be compact bushes, almost thornless, with dark green leaves; they flower for two or three weeks in June. The flowers have a light delicious fragrance that intensifies when dried, and consequently the petals are prized for potpourri. The 'Apothecary's Rose' (*R. gallica officinalis*) was esteemed in the Middle Ages not only for its scent but also for medicinal properties. On a low (three-foot) spreading bush, masses of large, brilliant, light crimson flowers, semidouble with yellow stamens, make a gorgeous display. Its sport, 'Rosa Mundi' (*R. gallica versicolor*), is the best of the striped roses. The same large semidouble petals are splashed and ribboned with white and deep pink. Both of these striking roses grow in corners of the herb

'APOTHECARY'S ROSE'
(*Rosa gallica officinalis*)

garden, surrounded by the soft foliage of wormwood, lamb's-ears, and southernwood and bordered with thyme and spicy pinks. 'Tuscany Superb' is a stunning gallica with semidouble flowers of the deepest velvet crimson, showing golden stamens. It makes a fine picture in the main garden grouped with the white-variegated hosta 'Thomas Hogg' and early-blooming pale pink astilbes. The gallica 'Charles de Mills', with wonderfully swirled flowers of rich crimson-purple, is stunning in another length of border tangling with the blush-pink climber 'New Dawn' and dark green fronds of tansy.

The great Victorian shrub roses, the bourbons and hybrid perpetuals, are not reliably hardy for me, and over the years I have lost many of these beauties. Still, I enjoyed them greatly while they lasted, and would certainly recommend growing some of them if you have a sheltered spot or live in a slightly warmer zone. (There is rarely a winter here when the temperature does not plunge more than once to five or ten degrees below zero — often without the benefit of snow cover.)

The best and least expensive way to buy the old shrub roses is through mail-order catalogs. The bare-rooted plants look quite dead when they arrive in the beginning of April (or in November), but they are just dormant and in an ideal state for planting. If the garden beds are still squelchy, I heel the roses in by the compost heap, lying them flat in a shallow dug-out space, then covering them halfway with compost and soil. Well watered, they can remain in this state for a week or two until the garden soil is dry enough for planting. That first season they will produce few, if any, flowers, but the following June, masses of roses will be your reward.

It takes a few years for the old shrub roses to achieve their mature size (which is always bigger than you expected), so it is

best to allow more room than you think they will need, filling
in around them with annuals, biennials, or short-lived perennials until they are full grown. Many of these shrub roses need
some support when they bloom, for the weight of the numerous flowers tends to make the canes weep toward the ground.
Various kinds of props can be easily fashioned from branches
in your yard (locust and ash are good choices) and thrust into
the ground around the roses before they bloom.

Need I say that all the old roses are heavenly in bouquets?
They are like nineteenth-century paintings come to life, exquisite still lifes that you can touch and smell.

ॐ

COUNTERPOINTS

There are certain plants that I value in the June garden not
only for their individual beauty but also as vertical or linear
contrasts to all the floral roundness of the peonies and roses.

Foxgloves are perfect counterpoints, with their tall, graceful spires of drooping bells rising from broad basal clumps of
leaves. The common foxglove, *Digitalis purpurea*, a biennial, flourishes in the borders at Duck Hill. The long bell-
like flowers are mauve pink or creamy white, delightfully
speckled inside. They fall in racemes on one side of three- to
four-foot stems. (In some of the newer hybrids the flowers are
carried all the way around the stalk, but I rather prefer the
grace of the older kinds.) Though both colors of the common
foxglove are charming, the white forms are more effective
among the pink hues of the roses and peonies. Consequently I
cut down the stalks of the mauve-pink sorts as soon as the

FOXGLOVES
(*Digitalis purpurea*)

flowers have faded; the white foxgloves I allow to go to seed. Sometimes I cut the faded spikes when the seeds are ripe and wave them like a wand above the garden beds, scattering the tiny seeds where I want them to grow. By fall, small plants will have appeared with oval nubbly leaves. These will flower the following June. The plants that have finished flowering are pulled up and discarded in the fall or the following spring. Foxgloves like a soil rich in compost and well-rotted manure and will bloom in sun or shade, provided the soil is not baking-dry.

Baptisia australis is another marvelous vertical to combine with peonies and roses. In fact, it is a first-rate perennial at any time in the growing season and deserves a prominent place in the garden. It has handsome blue-green foliage and a neat, bushy habit of growth, rarely requiring staking. The flowers are pealike, borne loosely on three-foot spires, and are a most beautiful purplish blue. Baptisia is a big perennial, in maturity making a bush about three feet high and four feet wide. It is often seen in New England dooryards standing alone, shrub-like, or mingling with clumps of the old-fashioned lemon daylily (*Hemerocallis flava*), which blooms at the same time.

The gas plant or false dittany, *Dictamnus albus*, is another old-fashioned plant that complements the peonies and roses, with two- to three-foot spikes of elegant white flowers and attractive foliage that smells strongly of lemon peel. This perennial is a slow grower, taking a few years to reach its full size (a bushy two feet high and three feet wide), but it is undemanding and, like baptisia, its foliage remains good-looking throughout the season. It prefers a sunny position with room to develop, not overshadowed by shrubs or taller perennials. Here, in the herb garden, bushes of false dittany revel in the sunshine with lavenders and dwarf sage. Although the gas plant is poisonous, it is indeed an ancient herb, valued not only for its aromatic leaves and flowers but for the bark of its root, which was used medicinally. Two of its common names, gas plant and burning bush, refer to an inflammable oil, or gas, that the flower spikes give off. On a still, warm day, apparently, a lit match held to the flower spike will ignite the vapor, causing no harm to the plant. Besides the white-flowering variety, there is a rosy mauve kind (*D. albus* var. *purpureus*), which is attractive combined with pale yellows and white.

Veronica latifolia 'Crater Lake Blue' is a fairly small perennial that forms pleasing hummocks of green in early spring, then throws up two-foot racemes of stunning sapphire blue flowers in early June. Planted in front of pale pink peonies or mixed with lemon lilies and the thistlelike flowers of the perennial cornflower (*Centaurea montana*), it makes a nice picture. This veronica tends to sprawl at blooming time, so it is best to interlace small pieces of brushwood among the flower stems sometime before they bloom. After the flowers have faded, I shear the tops of the clumps to encourage new bushy growth.

The peach-leaved bellflower (or peachbells, as I have always known it), *Campanula persicifolia*, is a wonderful vertical to weave among the peonies and roses. It has two- to three-foot stems with racemes of delicate out-facing bells in white and a lovely lavender blue. If the faded bells are pinched off (this is sticky work, for the pedicels exude a white sap), this charming campanula will bloom for many weeks. It seems to benefit from frequent division and replanting in fresh soil enriched with compost, and will grow in either sun or partial shade.

Campanula lactiflora is another beautiful bellflower to combine with roses (it blooms a little late for the peonies). It does not quite qualify as a vertical, for it is broad in feeling rather

PEACHBELLS
(*Campanula persicifolia*)

than tall. It has three-foot stems carrying panicles of small bells that in my garden are a marvelous milky blue. Growing in stout clumps, it often needs staking with brushwood. Seedlings appear sometimes around the older plants, and these are cherished, for this perennial is an effective counterpoint in the June garden.

The tall delphiniums with six-foot spires of sky blue and purple and white are, of course, a traditional accompaniment to roses and like the same rich soil and sunshine. It is best, however, to grow them with good protection from the wind; a walled-in garden is ideal. I do not grow the great delphiniums at Duck Hill, for the hedges do not yet provide enough protection from the wind, and their heavy flower spikes would certainly snap in the first rainstorm. In our previous garden, which was backed by a high stone wall, delphiniums were a feature in June.

Iris provide splendid contrasts in the June garden. Their upright, swordlike leaves have a distinctive linear value, and their flowers, especially in the various blues and pale yellows and white, are perfect with peonies and roses.

The graceful Siberian iris (*Iris sibirica*) are my first choice for the mixed flower border. These really are "easy-care" perennials, requiring little or no attention after they are planted. Siberian iris form handsome clumps of arching grasslike leaves, and in mid- to late June throw up many heads of delicate flowers in lovely colors of lavender blue, purple, red-violet, and white. Unlike the bearded iris, Siberian iris will flower in partial shade as well as sun, do not need frequent division, and seem to be unbothered by pests and diseases. They are not only marvelous plants in the garden; I have seen them naturalized in a sunny meadow, where in June they created sheets of color in a soft medley of hues from purple to white.

A favorite bearded iris of mine, growing in the main garden, came to me as a gift from a friend years ago. I call it 'John's Blue'. It has smaller blooms but is more floriferous than any of my more modern varieties. The flowers are a telling, light lavender blue and smell strongly of grape juice. The leaves are a very gray green and stay healthy and effective without division much longer than the newer hybrids. I think 'John's Blue' is the old *Iris pallida* var. *dalmatica*.

In the herb garden, a clump of the Florentine iris is opening ghostly gray-white flowers that are sweetly scented. This is an ancient iris, valued for centuries as a source of orris root. The substance is extracted from its dried rhizomes and is still used today in the making of potpourri and perfume.

I have planted a few varieties of the dwarf *I. pumila* as a ground cover beneath some of the roses in the main garden. These cheerful, hardy iris bloom in May in shades of yellow and white and blue, but their small swordlike leaves remain a pleasant contrasting carpet under the roses in June.

❧

A

CERTAIN

CATERPILLAR

A gorgeous caterpillar appears at this season on the bushes of rue in the herb garden. He is psychedelic green with rings of black stripes down his length, each stripe decorated with a row of bright yellow dots. When touched, he shoots out brilliant orange horns, successfully scaring me every time. I lift him carefully off the rue (which will be stripped of leaves if he has his way) and transfer him unharmed to the compost heap. In the next phase of his life, he will be the elegant black swallowtail butterfly.

THE

HERB

GARDEN

IN

BLOOM

COTTAGE PINKS
(*Dianthus plumarius*)

Most of the year the herb garden is a muted symphony of grays and greens, relying on subtle harmonies and contrasts of foliage color and texture to achieve its special kind of beauty. But now, in June, it is full of color.

Pink and white rambling roses and creamy honeysuckle drape the arbor that shades a bench where I sit at the west end of the garden. From here I can survey all the color and drink in the heady mixture of fragrances on a sunny afternoon.

The creeping thymes that spill down the steps and carpet the gravel paths are studded with tiny mauve and pink and white flowers. Fragrant cottage pinks (*Dianthus plumarius*), with charming fringed flowers of white and rose pink rising above narrow tufts of blue-green foliage, edge the south-facing beds among the thymes. The lower-growing cheddar pinks (*D. gratianopolitanus*) tumble out of a south bed and into the path, a wave of small candy-pink single flowers that fill the air with spicy fragrance.

Bushes of lavender throw up masses of delicate per-fumed spikes above needlelike gray-green foliage. 'Munstead Dwarf', growing in compact clumps, is a soft lavender blue; 'Hidcote' is also compact, with flowers a deeper purple. Be-hind the lavender the false dittany bears racemes of white flowers among lemon-scented leaves. Catmint (*Nepeta* × *faassenii*) is a haze of lavender blue.

Allium moly spreads a patch of starry yellow under the striped gallica, 'Rosa Mundi'. Mauve tufts of chives and white feverfew flower with foxgloves near the ruffled pink damask rose 'Celsiana'. In the background, garden heliotrope (*Valeriana officinalis*) sends up soft clusters of fragrant white flowers on three-foot stems above deeply cut foliage.

In another bed the pearl-white flowers of Florentine iris mingle with the curious lilac spiked balls of *Allium christophii*. A few Madonna lilies planted by the arbor among clumps of glossy-leaved germander add a touch of elegance and heav-enly fragrance.

Brightest of all, the yarrows open disks of yellow flowers from pale yellow buds. *Achillea* 'Moonshine', a clear acid yellow with ferny gray foliage, is striking combined with the deep purple spikes of *Salvia* × *superba* 'East Friesland'. An-other splendid yarrow, 'Coronation Gold', is a deeper yellow. It has, I think, the best foliage among the yarrows — a pale gray-green that grows in lacy clumps and is, by itself, quite beautiful in the spring garden. Behind a drift of this yar-row, the pale lavender-blue flowers of *Salvia haematodes*, the meadow sage, make a pleasing picture. The great panicles of this biennial sage are handsome too with the chartreuse flowers of lady's mantle and the shocking pink blooms of the apothecary rose, *R. gallica officinalis*.

TWO

MODERN

ROSES

Once captivated by the charm and fragrance of the old shrub roses, I gradually gave up growing hybrid teas and floribundas. The old-time ramblers, too, have woven their way into my favor and are more evident at Duck Hill than the newer large-flowered climbers. But a few steadfast modern roses, shrub and climber, find places among the old-fashioned kinds in my garden. For two of these, especially, I am full of praise.

'Sea Foam' is a twentieth-century shrub rose that deserves to be better known. It makes a low, wide bush, three feet high and four feet wide, with handsome, glossy dark green foliage and stout thorny stems. At Duck Hill these roses gracefully clothe a low stone wall that divides the terrace from the herb garden above. Five bushes are planted in narrow beds at the foot of the wall and, beginning in mid-June, are covered with hundreds of small creamy-white double flowers. 'Sea Foam' continues to bloom all summer and will still be offering buds and flowers, now tinged with pink, in the late fall. (This is my

ROSE 'NEW DAWN'

husband's favorite rose to use as a boutonniere.) It has a light tea-rose scent.

'Sea Foam' and the rugosas, alone among my shrub roses, withstand the dreaded black spot in particularly wet and humid summers; and 'Sea Foam' is rarely visited by the voracious Japanese beetles. For some reason they are not overly attracted to the flowers, and its glossy foliage is a great deterrent; the beetles prefer to eat matte-finished leaves, which are more the rule among roses, certainly the majority of old roses. In early spring, when the forsythia is blooming, I prune the 'Sea Foam' bushes hard, cutting the canes back halfway and removing any weak-looking growth. Then I lace the beds with compost or well-rotted manure from the barn. After the first extravagant flush of bloom in late June, I spend a few hours deadheading the faded flowers, cutting just above the joint of a five or seven leaflet. 'Sea Foam' flourishes with this minimum of care. It makes a handsome, if thorny, hedge and is a dazzling sight during its long season of bloom.

'New Dawn' is a well-known modern climber that merits every bit of its popularity. A big climber with sturdy canes and good glossy dark green leaves, it has large double hybrid tea–like flowers of a beautiful pale blush pink. It is hardy and disease-free and blooms fairly steadily all summer and into fall. With help it will climb a wall or trellis, but at Duck Hill I allow it to grow as a shrub. Its great arching canes wind among the branches of some gallica roses and fronds of fern-leaf tansy nearby. The pale pink blooms are wonderful mingled with the rich crimson of the gallicas; and 'New Dawn' continues to bloom against a background of deep green long after the older roses have stopped. In September the tall aster 'Alma Potschke' comes up through the canes of this marvelous climber, and the gaudy pink daisies mix nicely with the last pearly blooms of the rose.

༬

GRAY
IN THE
GARDEN

Gray-leaved plants add a special beauty to the garden, enhancing most flower colors and contrasting splendidly with all the various shades of green. For me, they are an essential element in the mixed border or formal garden, more important than the fleeting colors of flowers, adding a uniquely rich, soft light to the scene.

Three perennials stand out as stars among gray-leaved plants: lamb's-ears (*Stachys byzantina*), *Artemisia ludoviciana* 'Silver King', and lavender cotton (*Santolina chamaecyparissus*). Lamb's-ears is indispensable as a front-of-the-border

LAMB'S-EARS
(*Stachys byzantina*)

perennial. It plays an important part in the pattern of my garden beds, for its silvery, feltlike leaves make a striking statement wherever they are used. Short, wide stretches of lamb's-ears mark either side of the entrances to the little white garden. Here I have used many gray-green plants, for they are lovely combined with white flowers (and touches of lavender blue), and create handsome contrasts with the darker greens of boxwood and astilbe, cranesbills and lungwort. The four inside corners of the herb garden are planted with carpets of lamb's-ears to accentuate the formal pattern. Clumps of alliums and frothing lady's mantle are delightful companions, and the pink roses blooming above the lamb's-ears are enhanced by the carpet of gray.

Corresponding stretches of lamb's-ears are effective in the main garden, too, with lavender catmint and the pink cranesbills and dwarf bearded iris. I cut off the woolly flowering stalks in late June, preferring the carpet of leaves alone, although the curious mauve flower spikes are loved by bees (I have been stung while cutting them down) and valued by flower arrangers. There is a sterile cultivar of lamb's-ears that does not flower, called 'Silver Carpet'. I have another variety of lamb's-ears with larger leaves, which also does not bloom and is quite handsome, but the color is not as silver (more of a soft gray-green) and therefore is not quite as effective.

Artemisia 'Silver King', as I have mentioned, lends a lush romantic air to the garden with its billows of white-green foliage. A middle or back-of-the-border plant, it echoes the color of the lamb's-ears at the garden's front edge. It has deeply cut ferny leaves and inconspicuous panicles of gray-white flowers in late summer. It is a marvelous plant to cut and dry for winter arrangements and is often used as a base for herbal wreaths. *Artemisia* 'Silver Queen' is similar in color and habit but with slighter, broader leaves.

The shrubby herb gray santolina (or lavender cotton) has the same silver foliage, a green so pale that it is almost white. The plant has curious corallike leaves, a pungent fragrance, and a splendid habit of growth, forming dense, round clumps about a foot high. It is ideal for the front edge of the border, enhancing the flowers and greenery above it with its pale, structured mounds. Sadly, in our New York climate, with its extremes of humidity and heat, santolina is vulnerable to a soil-borne fungus that rapidly kills it off. A sandy soil in full sun is best for growing lavender cotton, and it is well worth the effort and gamble, for no other plant quite replaces its rich mounds of silver in the garden.

Artemisia schmidtiana 'Silver Mound' is sometimes suggested as a substitute for lavender cotton. It does have low-growing mounds of silvery green foliage (not quite as gray as santolina), lacy and attractive in its youth. But by midsummer this artemisia tends to collapse and sprawl, losing much of its effectiveness. It needs to be sheared to encourage new sturdy growth.

LAVENDER COTTON
Santolina chamaecyparissus

A number of other good perennials and shrubs have gray-green foliage — not quite the silver of lamb's-ears or lavender cotton or *A.* 'Silver King', perhaps, but with a paleness that is pleasing and effective in the garden. *Nepeta × faassenii* is a superb example, having small pebbly leaves of pale green that grow in bushy mounds. With its sprays of lavender flowers, it makes a lovely edging for roses, and in or out of bloom, it blends with and complements all the soft colors in the garden.

Cottage pinks (*Dianthus plumarius*), with their fat tufts of gray-green leaves, have the same effect. They form good clumps where the situation suits them, in full sun and a sandy soil sweetened with lime or wood ashes.

Lavender is another striking gray-green plant flourishing in the same conditions as cottage pinks with protection from bitter winds. In winter the shrubby bushes turn a pale leaden gray.

Some of the yarrows have good gray-green foliage and form attractive clumps where they have plenty of sun and space. The sages, too, offer some handsome pale foliage. The cooking sage (*Salvia officinalis*) and its dwarf variety are valuable in the garden for their pleasant mounds of pebbly gray-green leaves that stay fresh-looking until frost. *S. argentea* makes a rosette of large woolly leaves with a silver cast to them and is a striking accent in a border. Wormwood (*Artemisia absinthum*) throws up great stalks of feathery pale green and is a pleasing mass of foliage in the background of a herb or flower bed.

The fall-blooming *Caryopteris × clandonensis* is a lovely small shrub for the perennial border, with upright branches of pale gray-green leaves enhanced by soft blue flowers in September. Russian sage, *Perovskia atriplicifolia*, another shrubby plant, has wispy branches of silver leaves and spikes of lavender blue in late summer.

Next to pale gray foliage (and not counting green), I think the flower color lavender blue, even more than white, complements and harmonizes with all the other colors in the garden; the one exception is with the warm blood reds. Although both gray and lavender-blue are beautiful with crimson and clear scarlet, I do not like their effect with strong rust reds. The blood reds and orange reds, I think, are best combined with copper- and burgundy-hued foliage, rich greens, and yellow flowers ranging from pale cream to gold.

❧

SOME
RAMBLERS

Rambling roses differ from large-flowered climbers in having many lax, supple canes and a profusion of small flowers usually borne in clusters. They are perfect for clothing arbors, tumbling over stone walls, or clambering up the side and over the roof of a small building. Some of the most rampant kinds are thrilling to see fountaining down from an old tree whose limbs they have climbed. In the fields around Duck Hill, the vigorous Japanese rose, *Rosa multiflora*, with its masses of small fragrant white flowers, weaves through abandoned fruit trees and tumbles from dense olive green columns of Eastern red cedar.

At Duck Hill, 'Félicité et Perpétue' is the first rambler to bloom, in early June. It is an exquisite rose with clusters of small creamy white double flowers, often tinged with blush pink, opening from tiny pink buds. It has been trained up and over the west side of an arbor that marks the entrance to the vegetable garden. Graham Stuart Thomas recommends growing 'Félicité et Perpétue' as a wide mounding bush (which I have successfully done) or over a low wall or a tree stump: but it is equally delightful here frothing from the arbor, where it mingles with the autumn-blooming clematis (*C. paniculata*) and a bright rose-pink rambler called 'Alexander Girault', which climbs up and meets it from the other side.

'Alexander Girault' blooms slightly later and lasts until the end of June, clothing the east side of the arbor with glossy dark green leaves and a brilliant cloud of double flowers that are somewhere between pink and scarlet in color. They are full-petaled but open flat to reveal centers touched with white and yellow. This is a healthy and vigorous rose with almost no thorns and a light, pleasing fragrance.

Sharing the herb garden arbor with the white-flowering climber 'Silver Moon' is another charming rambler with soft coloring called 'Trier'. This bushy rose has lovely clusters of creamy white semidouble flowers with golden centers. The profuse buds are often tinged with blush pink. This rose is apparently one of the parents of the lovely twentieth-century group of roses called hybrid musks, which in habit are halfway between shrubs and climbers.

'Complicata' is classed as a gallica, not a rambler, but with its long lax canes and semiwild look it resembles the old-time climbers and species more than the ancient shrub roses. The flowers are large and single, bright warm pink fading to white at their centers and having there a mass of golden stamens. This striking rose is best grown away from the magenta-pink roses, for the color of 'Complicata,' perhaps because of the prominent golden boss of stamens, has a hint of coral to it. In the main garden it is allowed to arch about groups of *Artemisia* 'Silver King' and summer phlox. In England, at Mottisfont Abbey's garden of old roses, I have seen 'Complicata' clambering up and over a fruit tree some twenty feet high in one of the borders.

In late June, as the old shrub roses are fading, the star of my garden is a rambling rose that climbs up the side of our kitchen and fountains in wild profusion from the low roof toward the terrace below. I believe it is an old American rambler called 'Hiawatha'. For several weeks it is covered with hundreds of small scarlet-pink single flowers with white centers.

I found this rose growing weakly in a semiwild state at the top of a wall at our old home, completely shaded by some tall oak trees. Noticing that it had charming small flowers, I brought a root of it with us to Duck Hill; thinking that it might indeed be a rambler, I planted it next to the vigorous old climber 'Dr. W. Van Fleet' against the south wall of our newly built kitchen. In two years' time it had grown lustily up

RAMBLER 'HIAWATHA'

the wall and bloomed profusely, to my delight intertwining with the large blush flowers of the 'Van Fleet'. In five years 'Hiawatha' had crossed the roof, throwing flowering wands down from its height and transforming our kitchen ell into a bower. Now 'Dr. W. Van Fleet' has almost given up competing with it, and I know I must seriously tackle this lusty rambler with pruning shears after it finishes blooming. This will be a daunting and thorny task — I shall wear my waxed, scratch-proof rain jacket and stout leather gloves, and choose a day that is not too hot, when I am feeling particularly courageous and energetic. The reward will be a certain suggestion of order and plenty of new young growth for next year's display.

I think there is nothing more romantic or inviting in a garden than a profusion of ramblers framing a place to walk or to sit and muse.

❧

CORALBELLS
AND
FLAX

Some perennials are so delicate as to seem insignificant in the lavishness of the June garden. Yet they add a lightness and charm that should not be underestimated. Louise Beebe Wilder calls them flowers of grace, the butterflies of the flower garden.

Coralbells (*Heuchera* × *brizoides*), with their fragile-looking sprays of tiny bells, are a good example. They are in full bloom through much of June among the great peonies and roses, iris and baptisias, and their dancing bells add a lovely lightness and grace to the scene. The attractive, kidney-shaped leaves grow in small mounds, ideal for the front border of the garden. The racemes of bells are held well above the foliage on wiry stems. Several clumps of coralbells to-gether make the best effect, and in early spring they can be easily pulled apart to make new plants. They prefer a humus-rich soil and will grow in either sun or light shade. The colors of the bells range from pink to scarlet to white. 'Chatterbox' is a good pink variety grown here in the main garden. 'Pluie de Feu' is brighter in color, a lively scarlet. The variety 'White Cloud' has creamy white bells and lighter green leaves. It dances delicately with lavender sprigs of catmint in front of a clump of white bearded iris in the white garden.

Blue flax, *Linum perenne*, is another flower of grace in the

CORALBELLS
(*Heuchera* × *brizoides*)

June garden, with delicate dime-sized flowers that are the color of the sky on a clear day. This is a winsome, fleeting perennial, the dainty five-petaled flowers opening with the morning sun and closing by midday. They are held a foot or more high on waving wiry stems above insignificant slender foliage. The plants can be inserted among the stouter perennials in the borders, where they take up almost no room but add an enchanting lightness to the garden.

Blue flax prefers a sunny, well-drained position; although short-lived, it will seed around prettily in the garden. There is a yellow flax (*L. flavum*) that I have not grown, and another blue flax, *L. narbonense*, which is said to be more substantial and longer blooming than *L. perenne*, though not quite as hardy. Both *L. perenne* and *L. narbonense* have white-flowering forms.

WHAT GROWS IN THE GRAVEL

The gravel paths in the herb garden are host to a wide assortment of young plants that enjoy seeding there from the adjoining beds. Seedlings of lady's mantle and germander, hyssop and cottage pinks appear in the gravel below the beds and are carefully dug up and planted in nursery rows, where they soon become lusty full-sized plants. The biennial meadow sage and clary sage start life in the paths and are quickly lifted and planted in the garden beds before they get big, for they have fleshy taproots and become difficult to move successfully. Annuals seed in the gravel too, love-in-a-mist (*Nigella damascena*) and the chartreuse-flowered nicotiana and Johnny-jump-ups. Most of these are moved to the garden beds (I use a small clam knife for the operation); a few are left to grow where they have sown.

Best of all, the various creeping thymes seed and spread in the gravel paths, and I allow these to stay, for they are unharmed by foot traffic, and their aromatic mats of gray and green soften the gravel. The various forms of *Thymus serpyllum*, sometimes called mother-of-thyme, are the smallest in leaf; they hug the ground and pour over stones and brick into the gravel. *T. serpyllum coccineus* has crimson flowers and tiny dark green leaves. The variety 'Albus' has lighter green leaves and dainty white flowers in June. There is a delicious lemon-scented kind with tiny dark green leaves and mauve flowers, and a golden-variegated variety called 'Doone Valley'. Woolly thyme (*T. serpyllum lanuginosus*) is a lovely pale

CREEPING THYME
(*Thymus serpyllum*)

gray-green with a furry look to it. 'Halls Woolly' thyme has dark red stems and green leaves with a fuzzy texture and pretty lavender flowers. Caraway thyme (*T. herba-barona*) is leggier, with wiry stems and larger dark green leaves and a particularly delicious scent. All the thymes revel in the sunshine and good drainage provided by the stone steps and gravel of the paths.

While I am working in the herb garden, the two small white dogs, my constant companions, curl up on the nearby mats of thyme (woolly thyme is preferred), assuming, I think, that these soft ground covers are blankets laid out especially for them.

Corsican mint (*Mentha requienii*) creates small pools of bright green in the half-shaded gravel area by the arbor. The tiny round shiny leaves of this mint have an amazing fragrance — when rubbed, they smell just like the cordial crème de menthe.

The lacy white-flowered fumitory, *Corydalis ochroleuca*, froths in the gravel of the terrace below the herb garden. Here, too, the old-fashioned catmint, *Nepeta mussinii*, seeds freely in the spring and is a pretty picture with the corydalis and patches of Johnny-jump-ups and blue violas.

Brick paths and brick terraces also may be hosts to a charming company of self-seeders. White and bright crimson maiden pinks (*Dianthus deltoides*) spread down the old brick path between the main garden and the house and are a sparkling picture when in flower in June. This is a tough, hardy *Dianthus* that makes a good ground cover, with mats of tufted dark greenery and a profusion of small flowers that are curiously scentless.

The fragrant annual white sweet-alyssum creates a light-hearted scene in a garden nearby, where it has been allowed to seed and romp among the bricks of a terrace bordered by beds of roses and pansies and great old bushes of box.

July

IN DEFENSE OF HERB GARDENS

LAVENDER
(*Lavandula angustifolia*)

Christopher Lloyd, in his column for *Country Life*, once described herb gardens as sentimental messes. He went on to say, in his book *The Well-Chosen Garden*, that most herbs are "weeds at heart" and that "a herb garden, unless minded by the strictest custodians . . . quickly dissolves into an uncontrolled mess. This is made the more likely from the fact that the majority of herbs enthusiasts are congenitally untidy people anyway!"

I protest! I can think of a couple of dozen fellow herb enthusiasts in the New York area alone who have tidy gardens and houses — tidy without sacrificing charm, the pleasurable signs of living, and comfort. And although a number of herbs are weedy (the mints, of course, come immediately to mind), there are as many nonweedy kinds that stay good-looking all summer. Perfect examples are the shrubby herbs like germander and lavender, green and gray santolina, rue, southernwood, and the ornamental sages.

Some herbs that I would not necessarily call weedy do tend to spill and sprawl by midsummer, like the thymes and

137

oreganos and winter savory. Because of this, I think a formal geometric pattern works best; the spilling herbs are then a pleasing contrast to the strict lines of the garden. And if you are careful to keep the more rampant herbs in check and to mix the spilling herbs with more structurally upright sorts, if your pattern of beds is kept clearly delineated, accented by bushes of box, perhaps, or a sundial or a seat, there is no reason why a herb garden cannot be beautiful all season.

The herb garden at Duck Hill is more ornamental than useful, enjoyed primarily for its patterns and textures and fragrances. The herbs we use most for cooking are grown in the vegetable garden, where my husband (who is the chef in our kitchen) can snip and shear without disturbing a garden picture. A large clump of lavender is kept there too, and I cut the developing flower spikes in their prime to dry and scent our linen drawers or to mix with rose petals and lemon verbena for a potpourri. The lavender bushes in the herb garden, on the other hand, are left to bloom without cutting, their masses of flower spikes contributing beauty and fragrance to the overall scene.

Here in New York, I think a herb garden is at its peak in July. The shrubby herbs are full grown, rich and billowy and often studded with flowers; the differing colors of green (yellow-hued, silver, or glaucous blue) are at their most vibrant; and in the baking heat, the air is heady with a mixture of pungent and sweet scents.

Fred McGourty, writing in his fine book on perennials about the renewed popularity of culinary herbs, remarks that "herbs have come a long way since the 1940s, and the herb garden is no longer the preserve of slightly dotty, generally harmless old women whose closets smell of lavender sachets."

(I have learned everything I know about herbs and herb gardening from those "dotty" old women. I suppose I am at risk one day of being so described myself.) He goes on to repeat Christopher Lloyd's warning that a herb garden gets messy by midsummer and recommends instead combining the better-behaved herbs with perennials and annuals in the flower garden.

I agree wholeheartedly that herbs with good foliage should be used more in the mixed border, as they are in English gardens. But when critics like Christopher Lloyd and Fred McGourty dismiss herb gardens, they are forgetting two things: first, that it is fun, for a change, to have a place where flowers are incidental, where the beauty is in the pattern of the garden and the variety of foliage shapes and colors and scents; and second, that if herbs are merely dispersed among other plants, you lose the power of their interwoven scents. In an enclosed herb garden, there is a unique and wonderful concentration of fragrance on a hot summer day that is unlike anything else I know. It is a combination, I think, of sun-baked thyme and santolina, boxwood and lavender, southernwood and pinks that is unforgettably heady and thrilling. This, to me, is the best, most rewarding reason for a herb garden.

Why, I wonder, are most creators of herb gardens women? All the best herb gardens that I am familiar with, here and in England, have been designed and planted by women. Is it possible that fragrance in the garden is more important to women than it is to men?

Recently a blind man came to visit my herb garden. We walked slowly along the paths, pausing as I pinched off leaves of various herbs for him to rub and smell. Balsam-scented thyme; tansy, with its strong odor of crushed ferns; hyssop, smelling slightly of skunk; lemon thyme and lemon verbena, so redolent of lemon candy; lavender, fragrant in both leaves and flowers; rosemary with its intense oily aroma of pine; the sharp acrid smell of rue; pungent santolina and the southern-woods — the camphor-scented one and the more common fruity kind; aromatic wild marjoram; oregano, conjuring up thoughts of pizza; the licorice smell of sweet cicely and anise hyssop; pineapple sage, truly smelling of that fruit; and, of course, the mints — delicious ginger mint and the sharper-scented apple mint, orange mint smelling deeply of orange, and the tiny Corsican mint with its astonishing peppermint odor, like sniffing a cordial glass of crème de menthe.

Children (even teenagers) are intrigued and delighted with this garden. Unabashed, sensual creatures, they love being encouraged to touch and smell. My offspring, now grown up, still enjoy milling about the herb garden with their friends, as they did when they were young, pinching and smelling, identifying and comparing the endlessly varied scents of the herbs.

❦

ROOSTERS

We have a Japanese fan-tailed rooster who, with his favorite small hen, refuses to go into the hen house at night, preferring instead to roost in the rafters of the barn above the horses. This is a very secure place to sleep, safe from marauding raccoons and foxes (and coyotes) who check often, I am sure, to see if we have forgotten to latch the chicken-house door. (Once or twice over the years we have indeed forgotten, or a raccoon has pried the door open, resulting in a massacre.)

JAPANESE
FAN-TAILED
ROOSTER

COCHIN ROOSTER, CROWING

ENGLISH GAME COCK

However, our fan-tailed rooster wakes up very early in the morning, before the sun rises, in fact, and he has taken to coming to the garden by our bedroom window to crow. We are early risers, but 4:30 A.M. is too early, and I wish he would stay with our other roosters in their house, where any attempt to crow before we get up and let them out is nicely muffled.

Roosters, like people, have distinct voices and are easily told apart by their crowing. Our giant pantalooned Cochin rooster has a deep sonorous crow. On the other hand, the voice of our tiny English game cock is predictably high-pitched. The crow of the Japanese fan-tail, I am sorry to say, is rather abrupt and screeching. (He is, nevertheless, an elegant creature, with striking black and white feathers that sweep up and over his small plump white body in an arc; he is very low-slung, his breast almost touching the ground.)

All roosters put their heart and soul into crowing. They swell up, arch their necks, take a deep breath, stand on their toes, and let go with everything they have. This is usually followed by a shake of the feathers and a few minutes of rest, sometimes by a quick-stepping circular dance around a favorite hen, the inside wing flirtatiously dropped to the ground. Then they gear up again for another crow.

It is a myth that roosters crow only at daybreak. They crow off and on all day until dusk, reaffirming their virility and their command among the hens in the barnyard. As I garden, I hear distant roosters echoing ours from a circle of neighboring farms across the fields.

※

DAYLILIES

Daylilies (varieties of *Hemerocallis*) are the mainstay of the July garden. Although some kinds bloom as early as May and some as late as October, they are in their glory in July, and to my mind they are an essential ingredient of the midsummer flower border. Daylilies are endlessly accommodating, growing well in either sun or light shade, untroubled by diseases or the vagaries of our weather. (Alas, deer enjoy browsing the emerging leaves and flower buds, so in areas like ours some deterrent is necessary — dried blood sprinkled on the ground or an anti-deer spray or, best of all, a seven-foot-high wire fence!) Daylilies bloom for many weeks and do not require frequent division, the clumps growing fuller and more handsome with age. On the other hand, if you want to extend a certain variety, it can be easily propagated by pulling apart the tuberlike roots in early spring or fall.

There are now a dizzying number of hybrid daylilies to choose from. Colors range from the palest yellow through all the variations of lemon and gold, apricot, orange, pink, and rose, culminating in the dense, dark blood reds. Shapes of the flowers and their heights vary too, and I think if you are starting out to buy daylilies, it is advisable to go first to a botanical garden or nursery where they are in bloom to see what colors and styles appeal to you.

In the main garden at Duck Hill, where we have so many candy-pink and mauve-pink flowers, I have planted daylilies that are clear yellow in color, with no hint of orange or gold. My favorite is an old stalwart called 'Hyperion'. It is a handsome daylily with gracefully arching straplike leaves and tall, simple, fragrant trumpets of pure lemon yellow. It is hardy

DAYLILY 'HYPERION'

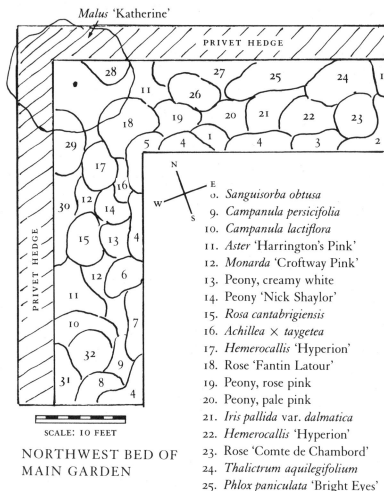

Malus 'Katherine'

PRIVET HEDGE

PRIVET HEDGE

SCALE: 10 FEET

NORTHWEST BED OF MAIN GARDEN

1. Chrysanthemum, cushion type, pink
2. *Iris pumila*, yellow
3. *Coreopsis* 'Moonbeam'
4. *Nepeta* × *faassenii*
5. *Alchemilla mollis*
6. Bearded iris, pale yellow
7. *Stachys byzantina*

8. *Sanguisorba obtusa*
9. *Campanula persicifolia*
10. *Campanula lactiflora*
11. *Aster* 'Harrington's Pink'
12. *Monarda* 'Croftway Pink'
13. Peony, creamy white
14. Peony 'Nick Shaylor'
15. *Rosa cantabrigiensis*
16. *Achillea* × *taygetea*
17. *Hemerocallis* 'Hyperion'
18. Rose 'Fantin Latour'
19. Peony, rose pink
20. Peony, pale pink
21. *Iris pallida* var. *dalmatica*
22. *Hemerocallis* 'Hyperion'
23. Rose 'Comte de Chambord'
24. *Thalictrum aquilegifolium*
25. *Phlox paniculata* 'Bright Eyes'
26. Rose 'Common Moss'
27. *Artemisia abrotanum*
28. *Geranium endressii*
29. *Thalictrum glaucum*
30. *Artemisia* 'Silver King'
31. Japanese anemone 'September Charm'
32. Rose 'Felicité Parmentier'

NOTE:
Crabapples and roses underplanted with *Pulmonaria angustifolia*.

and floriferous and very effective in the garden, having good structure and a telling color. A nurseryman recently tried to persuade me to buy a "new improved" dwarf version of 'Hyperion'. It was useless to explain that it is in the height of the blooms (to about three feet) that this fine old variety achieves its gracefulness. Many of the newer daylilies are dumpy in comparison and not nearly as effective as garden plants. I prefer, too, the simple star-shaped trumpets to the fleshy, wide-petaled, ruffled sorts.

Several golden yellow daylilies, whose names I have long since confused and lost, bloom in clumps in the terrace beds below the herb garden. They are pleasant here in July with the white 'Sea Foam' roses and spikes of white peachbells and the creamy white fumitory (*Corydalis ochroleuca*) that froths from the walls and into the gravel. In the nasturtium border, gold and orange and apricot daylilies blend together nicely around bushes of *Viburnum opulus* 'Compactum' (its fruit just starting to color) and the ruby-leaved purple barberry, with calendulas and purple sage grouped below them.

At the edge of the woods and all along the roadsides, the burnished orange blooms of the tawny daylily (*H. fulva*) are out in profusion, making a handsome display. This species has naturalized widely in our area and is a gladdening sight as early as March, when its emerging leaves clothe the banks and roadways with light green in a landscape that is still brown and gray. It makes an excellent ground cover below shrubs and deciduous trees that cast a light shade.

I have two double-flowered daylilies in the July garden. One, a relative of *H. fulva*, is a tall-stemmed, burnished coppery flower, large and full of petals, called 'Kwanso'. It starts to bloom in late July and is a striking addition to the nasturtium border, mingling with the first black-eyed Susans.

In an old garden I once saw 'Kwanso' used as a ground cover around a blue pool framed with flowering shrubs and dogwood trees.

The other double-flowered daylily is a charming variety called 'Cheek to Cheek'. It is pale lemon yellow, rather ruffled with petals, looking almost like a double daffodil. It blooms among fringed bleeding hearts and variegated hosta in a corner of the main garden.

꙳

SOME
ASTILBES

A fine contrast to daylilies, astilbes are marvelous plants for the summer garden, thriving in light shade and a moist, humus-rich soil. Their delicate ferny foliage is always presentable, and their feathery plumes of flowers, ranging from white to pink to crimson, are striking and effective in the mixed flower border or planted in drifts through light woodland. They are the easiest plants in the world to increase by division in the spring, so one purchased plant can quickly be made into many.

'Deutschland', the first astilbe to bloom at Duck Hill, opening in late June, is a low-growing variety with creamy white plumes that stand upright. 'Avalanche' is taller-growing (two to three feet) with gracefully arching panicles of white flowers, in their prime in mid-July. These two varieties are woven through the beds of the white garden, flowering with cranesbills and blue catmint and spires of white mullein.

The tallest white astilbe I have, blooming in mid-July, is 'Professor van der Weilen'. This is a four-footer with arching cream-white plumes, suitable for the back of a lightly shaded border. Here, in the main garden, it mixes nicely with dark green fernleaf tansy (*Tanacetum vulgare* 'Crispum') and the elegant trumpet lily 'Moonlight Strain'.

'Peach Blossom' is not peach at all, but a pretty pale pink. It is low-growing and blooms here in July with deeper pink fringed bleeding hearts and lemon yellow daylilies. In contrast, 'Fanal' is a dark plum red, the flowers rising two feet above dark red-tinged foliage.

Astilbe taquetii 'Superba' extends the season of bloom from late July into August with tall, striking upright plumes of magenta pink. This handsome three- to four-foot plant can bring life to a shadowy place in the garden with its rockets of startling color.

The diminutive *A. chinensis* 'Pumila' ends the astilbe season at Duck Hill, flowering in late summer. It makes a good edging plant, with little spiky plumes, about a foot high, of lavender pink, the color of raspberry ice cream. It is, apparently, the astilbe most tolerant of dry soils.

ASTILBE 'PEACH BLOSSOM'

BIRD
SIGHTINGS

The gregarious purple finch and the gray mockingbird, full
of song, the chirping robin and softly cooing mourning dove,
the red cardinal calling "Cheer, cheer," and the chickadee —
these are my regular companions in the garden. Every summer barn swallows nest in the rafters of our barn, swooping in
and out during the day. All year long the red-tailed hawk
circles high above the garden and pasture, sometimes sound-
ing an eerie scream, often chased and bedeviled by smaller
birds.

Now and then, we catch glimpses of some rarer birds.
I often hear the whirring of his wings before I see the ruby-
throated hummingbird darting among the tiny bright pink
flowers of coralbells or the shaggy scarlet blooms of beebalm.
A pair of Baltimore orioles spends a day in the gnarled Scotch

BOUNCING BET
(*Saponaria officinalis*)

pine behind the herb garden, giving us flashes of their dramatic black and orange coloring.

I have been startled by the rapping noise of a pileated woodpecker as this huge bird works on an old dying tree in our sliver of woodland. Here, too, I hear the call of the bobwhite and sometimes the lovely trilling of a thrush.

Bluebirds come and go between the garden and the adjoining fields, fluttering patches of tropical cerulean blue. Small goldfinches, now in their brilliant lemon-yellow garb, flit by, briefly lighting on a berried shrub or clump of thistles, like fleeting flowers of summertime themselves.

BOUNCING BET

Bouncing Bet is blooming by roadsides and gateways, its clusters of fragrant phloxlike flowers a pale, pale pink. This old-time herb seems more suitable to the flower garden than the wayside; indeed, like so many of our summer wildflowers, it is not a native but a cultivated garden plant originally from Europe. Once a denizen of our gardens, it has escaped the boundaries of the flower border and become naturalized throughout our countryside. It is now more often considered a weed.

I would hesitate to include bouncing Bet in my flower garden no matter how appropriate it would look, for it is said to spread rapidly by underground stolons, and I have too many rampant flowers to contend with already. But it is lovely to see in the wild. There it is a charming partner for the

AT INSIDE CORNERS AND
AROUND VASE IN CENTER BED:
boxwood, *Buxus sempervirens* 'Suffruticosa'

THE WHITE GARDEN

1. *Stachys byzantina*
2. *Geranium sanguineum* 'Album'
3. *Astilbe* 'Deutschland'
4. *Phlox maculata* 'Miss Lingard'
5. *Liatris aspera* 'White Spires'
6. *Baptisia australis*
7. *Gypsophila paniculata*
8. *Digitalis purpurea*
9. *Artemisia* 'Silver King'
10. Peony 'Charlie's White'
11. *Verbascum chaixii* 'Album'
12. Japanese anemone 'Honorine Jobert'
13. Siberian Iris, white
14. *Linum perenne*
15. *Nepeta* × *faassenii*
16. *Heuchera* × *brizoides* 'June Bride'
17. *Veronica spicata* 'Icicle'
18. *Phlox paniculata* 'Mt. Fuji'

tawny daylily and white-flowering Queen Anne's lace, disks of white yarrow and sky-blue chicory. I often see it, too, in the dooryards of old New England farmhouses mingling with perennial sunflowers and hollyhocks.

The leaves and stems of bouncing Bet were once prized for the soapy lather they produce when crushed in water. Even today this natural detergent is valued in the restoration of old fabrics and tapestries. Hence its other common name, soapwort, and its Latin name, *Saponaria officinalis*.

THE WHITE GARDEN

For years I wanted a white garden. The romance and elegance of it appealed to me, and the challenge of painting a picture with a limited palette. Our climate, too, seemed per-

19. *Artemisia abrotanum*
20. *Rosa rugosa* 'Blanc Double de Coubert'
21. *Pulmonaria saccharata*
22. *Filipendula vulgaris* 'Flore Pleno'
23. *Astilbe* 'Avalanche'
24. *Chrysanthemum parthenium*
25. *Hosta sieboldiana* 'Elegans'
26. *Hosta* 'Royal Standard'
27. Peony 'Krinkled White'
28. *Lobelia siphilitica*
29. *Cornus alba* 'Elegantissima'
30. *Campanula persicifolia* 'Alba'
31. *Geranium macrorrhizum* 'Album'
32. *Boltonia asteroides* 'Snowbank'
33. *Potentilla fruticosa*, white
34. *Cimicifuga racemosa*
35. *Dicentra eximia* 'Alba'
36. *Caryopteris* × *clandonensis*
37. *Geranium* 'Johnson's Blue'
38. *Hosta* 'Louisa'

fect for a garden where the color is cool and restful on a hot summer's day. And at dusk — that magical time in the summer garden — the white flowers would shimmer with light and send wafts of fragrance into the evening air.

A small area between the main garden and the herb garden called for paths and garden beds as a link between the two larger gardens. Here I decided to give in to my folly and plant a white garden.

Two narrow bracket-shaped beds backed by a hedge of Japanese holly and a small center bed circled with boxwood and grass paths is all that the space could contain. It is a sheltered area, with full morning sun and dappled shade in the afternoon, which suits a variety of pale flowers. The garden is not nearly as large as I would like, but it is a pleasurable spot. And not only as a passageway to the other gardens. With a low sturdy table and two comfortable chairs at its west end, the white garden has become a favorite place to linger on a summer's day.

Not all the flowers are white. Touches of lavender blue and a hint of the creamiest yellow have been added to complement the various shades of white and ivory. Gertrude Jekyll writes splendidly on this subject in her book on color schemes:

> It is a curious thing that people will sometimes spoil some garden project for the sake of a word. For instance, a blue garden, for beauty's sake, may be hungering for a group of white lilies, or for something of palest lemon-yellow, but it is not allowed to have it because it is called the blue garden, and there must be no flowers in it but blue flowers. I can see no sense in this; it seems to me like fetters foolishly self-imposed. Surely the business of the blue garden is to be

beautiful as well as to be blue. My own idea is that it should be beautiful first, and then just as blue as may be consistent with its best possible beauty.

The early snowdrop, *Galanthus elwesii*, is the first flower to bloom in the white garden, often during a mild stretch of weather in early February. Shining chalices of the white Dutch crocus 'Jeanne d'Arc' follow in March, tucked around the emerging red buds of peonies. Silvery blue striped 'Pickwick' blooms here too, creating a pretty picture with the first pink buds and lavender flowers of spotted lungwort (*Pulmonaria saccharata*).

In April, the lungwort is in its prime, a haze of lavender-blue above its handsome white-spotted leaves. The early small daffodil 'February Silver' blooms at the same time, a lovely creamy flower, woven in small drifts around the perennials and shrubs at the back of the borders. White violas and Johnny-jump-ups are threaded among the burgeoning greenery of hostas and cranesbills near the front of the beds.

In May the lily-flowered tulip 'White Triumphator' takes the stage, creating an elegant picture among the rich greens and grays of the garden.

By the end of May, 'Blanc Double de Coubert', the double white rugosa rose, is blooming in the corners of the garden, large ruffled flowers that are richly fragrant. Baptisia opens its loose racemes of purply blue pealike flowers, and by the beginning of June, the peonies expand into large dishes of white satin petals with a boss of golden stamens. Siberian and bearded irises open their frilled white flowers touched with golden yellow, and nepeta throws up soft lavender sprays. Double dropwort (*Filipendula vulgaris* 'Flore Pleno') blooms handsomely in a corner. With its tall white plumes and dark green fernlike foliage, it is often mistaken for an early astilbe.

Clumps of foxgloves rise at the back of the borders and by mid-June are countered by the tall spikes of *Verbascum chaixii* 'Album'. This is a grand mullein with spires of small white flowers, each with a rosy eye. It is short-lived but seeds around in the garden, providing new blooming plants every year.

From the end of June through July, the white garden is at its peak. The early-flowering phlox 'Miss Lingard' is in full bloom, a stark white, the cylindrical flower heads contrasting nicely with the mist of nearby baby's breath (*Gypsophila paniculata*), the gray-white foliage of *Artemisia* 'Silver King', and the white-flowering spikes of *Liatris aspera*. The astilbes are now feathery plumes of cream and white. White coralbells dance above light green ruffled leaves, and the delicate white flowers of fringed bleeding hearts droop in a corner nearby.

The hardy geraniums, or cranesbills, are in their prime. *Geranium macrorrhizum* is here in its white-flowered form, 'Album', with rosy calyxes and buds. It is a splendid plant for

Geranium macrorrhizum 'ALBUM'

an edging in a moist, half-shaded place; the flowers are striking and the foliage provides a bold and pleasing contrast with
many perennials, in this instance the straplike foliage of Siberian iris. *G. sanguineum* 'Album' has smaller, darker leaves
and a looser habit of growth, with lovely sheer white five-
petaled flowers. *G.* 'Johnson's Blue' is a large hummock of a
plant with stunning lavender-blue flowers. It is showy here
beneath the silver-green leaves of the shrubby *Caryopteris*
with clumps of the dainty variegated hosta 'Louisa' in the
foreground.

White summer phlox is the main feature in August, deer
willing, with the soft blue spires of our native lobelia (*L.
siphilitica*) and the night-scented annual flowering tobacco
(*Nicotiana alata*).

In September the bluebeard, *Caryopteris* × *clandonensis*, is
misted all over with tufts of soft blue, and the handsome
Boltonia asteroides 'Snowbank' is a mass of asterlike flowers.
Shaggy white chrysanthemums are appreciated now. Last of
all to flower is the exquisite Japanese anemone 'Honorine
Jobert', tall-growing above clumps of compound dark green
leaves, opening pure, beautiful china-white flowers with
golden stamens.

In the center of the white garden is an old carved stone
vase, a present from dear friends, which I plant with violas in
the spring and variegated rose geraniums in the summer.
Around the base of the vase, *Nepeta* × *faassenii* is planted.
The May-flowering narcissus 'Silver Chimes' is tucked in
among the clumps of nepeta, and the bed is circled with small
plump bushes of dwarf box.

ɔ↰

BEEBALMS

The beebalms, or bergamots (*Monarda didyma* and its hybrids), add delightful splashes of color to the July garden. They are native American perennials with coarse dark green foliage that is deliciously mint-scented; the curious shaggy heads, really tiers of tubular flowers, seem to explode above a circle of colorful bracts.

Beebalm in its native form is a tall-growing plant with marvelous clear scarlet flowers beloved by hummingbirds. Here it grows appropriately in the herb garden (American colonists and Indians used the leaves to make tea), bringing a brilliant dash of color to a shadowy corner above white-flowering feverfew and sweet cicely.

'Croftway Pink' is a charming hybrid of beebalm with lighthearted candy-pink flowers. It looks wonderful combined with clear yellow daylilies and white and yellow garden lilies, as it is in our main garden; it blooms for many weeks, carrying on through July the pink color of June's roses and peonies.

After they finish blooming, the beebalms tend to look ratty, their leaves often splotched with mildew. I cut them back hard to encourage new fresh growth from the base. This, of course, creates a gap in the garden, so it is important to mask the beebalms with good surrounding foliage like that of the tall-growing asters or *Campanula lactiflora*, baptisia, or fern-leaf tansy. Beebalms respond well to division every few years (indeed, the scarlet beebalm seems to require it) but otherwise need no special care. Their leaves, when brushed in the spring, send up the most welcome fragrance, and for that reason alone they are a pleasure in the garden.

There is a white-flowered variety and several with lavender or violet flowers. *M. fistulosa* is the bergamot most usually seen in fields and in light woodland. It is not so tall-growing and has soft lavender-mauve flower heads.

❧

COOL
YELLOW
IN THE
MAIN
GARDEN

The color scheme of the main garden revolves around the color pink — the clear candy pinks and bluish pinks typical of the old roses. Lavender and purple flowers are here in quantity to complement the pink, and there is plenty of creamy white. Gray foliage is used to soften the picture, and crimson flowers to give it depth. But for a fillip, a hint of sunlight in the color scheme, I like to add touches of clear lemon yellow. Many yellow flowers, particularly in summer, tend toward golden and orange hues; but a number of perennials and bulbs can be found with the clear cool yellow tones that are so effective in a garden of candy pink and mauve.

In April and May the dabs of yellow in the main garden are provided by clumps of double daffodils; later by the early pale yellow roses, the rugosa 'Agnes' and *R. cantabrigiensis*.

In June a tall, very pale yellow bearded iris is an appealing picture planted in front of pink and crimson peonies and roses. It is echoed exactly in color by a clump of *Achillea × taygetea*. This is the only yarrow I know of with pale lemon-yellow flowers. It blooms through June and into July, and has

Thalictrum speciosissimum

foliage similar to that of 'Moonshine', a very gray green. 'Moonshine' is also a clear yellow with no gold in it, but it is a strong acid color, much brighter than *A.* × *taygetea*.

By the end of June, the tall, elegant *Thalictrum speciosissimum* is blooming. This meadow rue has blue-green columbinelike foliage and creamy yellow puffs of flowers held up high on graceful stems. It is a good perennial for the back of the border, reaching five to six feet in height. It flourishes if there is some dappled shade from the hot sun and if the soil does not get baking-dry.

Daylilies are probably the biggest source of lemon yellow for the garden; there are countless varieties to choose from with this coloring. In late May the old-fashioned lemon lily (*Hemerocallis flava*) opens small fragrant trumpets of clear yellow. These are a marvelous contrast to the iris and peonies and baptisia flowering at the same time. The July-blooming 'Hyperion', planted in drifts, supplies the main garden with clear yellow flowers for many weeks.

EVENING PRIMROSE
(*Oenothera fruticosa youngii*)

The cheerful evening primrose (*Oenothera fruticosa youngii*, now confusingly called *O. tetragona*) I allow to romp through the front borders of two beds. It has bright yellow saucer-shaped flowers opening from red-tinged buds. The leaves are dark green, often tinted with red. This is an easy, sunny flower to weave around stouter perennials, and it blooms for several weeks during the summer. After the evening primrose has finished blooming, I cut the flowering stems back to the ground. The low-growing rosettes of leaves that remain then become an attractive ground cover.

The true lilies, particularly the Asiatic hybrids, are excellent purveyors of clear yellow in the garden. If the bulbs are ordered by mail and planted in the fall, they can be tucked in closely among the existing perennials. (Peonies are a good choice, for their handsome leaves support and mask the tall stems of the lilies.) Lilies take up very little room in the garden, but they offer dramatic blocks of color and often last in bloom for several weeks. They do not thrive in a bed that is hot and baking, preferring a deep humusy soil that is well drained and protection from the heat of the sun for at least part of the day. 'Connecticut Lemonglow' with out-facing clear yellow flowers, and 'Edith', similar but lower-growing and nicely spotted, lighten shadowy spots in a border in June. The tall-growing 'Nutmegger', with numerous pendent recurved flowers, is a bright clear yellow. Groups of this lily enliven the sunny borders, flowering with pink beebalm for several weeks in July. 'Moonlight Strain', an elegant trumpet lily, is planted in semishade behind clumps of lavender-flowering *Hosta fortunei*. The fragrant trumpets are colored the palest yellow with a hint of chartreuse. The outside of the large petals is streaked with green.

Coreopsis verticillata 'Moonbeam' is a workhorse of a plant. It has a low mounded habit of growth, perfect near the front of the border, and is covered all summer with masses of small, rather delicate, daisylike flowers of a pale creamy yellow. It is not bothered by our summer heat or drought and will grow in either full sun or light shade. I would not go so far as to say that *Coreopsis* 'Moonbeam' is "one of the ten best perennials," as it is often described; it is just not interesting enough. The foliage is insignificant, and the daisy flowers ordinary. Nevertheless, I am grateful to have it in the garden, where its yellow is clear and telling, nice with stretches of lavender catmint and bright pink summer phlox; and where without any fuss, it blooms on and on through the summer.

᪥

HIGH
SUMMER

We are having a spell of hot sunny days, and all around Duck
Hill there is the sound of haying. It takes several days to cut
and turn and bale the hay in a field, and the trick is to finish
the work before it rains. It is always a gamble; an unexpected
thunderstorm can ruin a good hay crop in minutes.

The air throbs with the low humming of the tractors as
they crawl back and forth, methodically cutting the fields in
great parallel swaths. In a few hours, acres of waving green
grass are replaced by vast geometric patterns of golden beige
stripes. Rickety hay trucks are filled with the neatly squared
and tied bales and rumble past us, only to return later in the
day, emptied and ready for another load.

We turn our horses out at night now to graze in their
pasture. During the heat of the day, they remain in the barn,
which is cool and dark and catches any slight breeze coming
off the high fields.

The ducks and geese rely on buckets of water and a large
baby pool to refresh them in the heat. Every few days, to their
delight, we empty the pool and refill it with clear cold water.
The geese are always first to get in. With deliberate slow
movements, they dip their heads and necks in the fresh water
and splash with a great spread of wings. The ducks soon join
them and play submarine, swimming under water in dizzying circles; then they stretch and flap their wings, sending
water everywhere. After the swim, there is a good half hour
of preening. Working with their beaks and the backs of their
heads, they rub their feathers to restore the oils that help to

keep them waterproof. There is much flapping of wings, too, and standing on tiptoes, sometimes stretching a back leg out, like ballerinas doing their exercises. It is tempting to forget the garden and the chores and just stand at the barn door watching their antics.

In the vegetable garden, the tomatoes and basil and annual cutting flowers respond to the baking heat with a spurt of fresh growth.

August

CURLY CHIVES
(*Allium senescens glaucum*)

GOOD
FOLIAGE

HOSTAS

During the dog days of summer, neatness really counts in the garden. When you least feel like doing it, when the heat has sapped your energy and quelled your enthusiasm, staking, deadheading, weeding, and trimming are most needed to make the garden presentable. How easy it is, when the temperature hovers around ninety degrees and the sky is a white glare and the air throbs with the sound of locusts, to turn your back on the garden, give up, go inside where it is cool, hope for better days. But then the weeds march into the beds, quickly gaining the upper hand, and before you know it the garden takes on a jungle look that is not at all what you had in mind.

It is now that I most appreciate good foliage in the garden. If plenty of plants with healthy, shapely foliage are included in the scheme, it is infinitely easier to keep the garden tidy and attractive in high summer. (This is particularly important, I think, along the front of the borders, where plants with good foliage create a long-lasting frame for incidental flowers behind.)

Hostas are an excellent example. As a front edging for the garden in half-shaded areas, they put on a marvelous show all summer, making a bold structural statement with their handsomely shaped and colored leaves. I particularly like the silver-variegated hostas like 'Thomas Hogg' and *H. fortunei marginato-alba*, or the small-leaved 'Louisa', in shadowy places; they almost seem like bouquets of flowers themselves. *H. sieboldiana* 'Elegans' is a dramatic kind with immense blue-green leaves that are heart-shaped and ribbed with a texture that makes them look quilted. This is a grand hosta to punctuate a corner of the garden. It unfurls in spring like skunk cabbage, and a single plant, after a few years, develops into a clump about four feet wide. 'Frances Williams' is another show-stopper with the same huge quilted leaves, this time dipped and edged in yellow-green.

The solid green hostas, like *H. plantaginea* and its handsome cultivar 'Royal Standard', are every bit as useful in the garden, contrasting well with grasslike clumps of daylilies and Siberian iris and the intricate leaves of cranesbills and astilbes. Three plants together are enough to make a generous grouping.

As a bonus, all of these hostas flower in July or August, sending up stalks of drooping bells in white or lavender blue that are often pleasantly fragrant. The one drawback to hostas in our area is that they are relished by the deer; unless a fence or spray or other anti-deer device is used to deter these vandals, the flowers and foliage will be munched until they are no longer decorative in the garden. (How discouraging it is, on a fine summer morning, to come out and find the tattered remains of a particularly handsome stand of hosta!)

Baptisia australis is another example of top-notch foliage for the garden and, happily, it is deer-proof. Its bushy habit

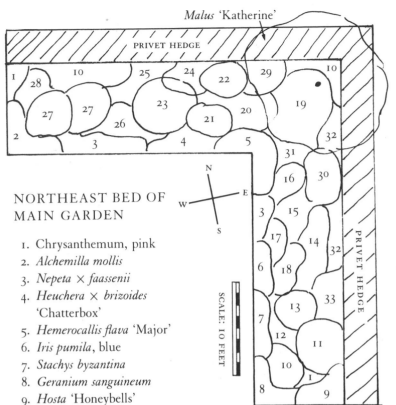

Malus 'Katherine'

PRIVET HEDGE

PRIVET HEDGE

N
W ——E
S

NORTHEAST BED OF MAIN GARDEN

SCALE: 10 FEET

1. Chrysanthemum, pink
2. *Alchemilla mollis*
3. *Nepeta* × *faassenii*
4. *Heuchera* × *brizoides* 'Chatterbox'
5. *Hemerocallis flava* 'Major'
6. *Iris pumila*, blue
7. *Stachys byzantina*
8. *Geranium sanguineum*
9. *Hosta* 'Honeybells'
10. *Hemerocallis* 'Hyperion'
11. Rose 'Madame Hardy'
12. *Oenothera tetragona*
13. *Rose* 'Camaieux'
14. *Phlox paniculata* 'Gaiety'
15. *Monarda* 'Croftway Pink'
16. *Echinacea purpurea*
17. *Veronica latifolia* 'Crater Lake Blue'
18. Peonies, pale pink, double
19. *Phlox divaricata*
20. *Ruta graveolens*
21. Rose 'Autumn Damask'
22. Rose 'Queen of Denmark'
23. *Syringa meyeri* 'Palibin'
24. *Geranium macrorrhizum*
25. *Phlox* 'Starfire'
26. Bearded iris, pale blue
27. Rose 'Jacques Cartier'
28. Peony 'Scarlet O'Hara'
29. *Baptisia australis*
30. Rose 'Complicata'
31. *Centaurea montana*
32. *Artemisia* 'Silver King'
33. *Artemisia abrotanum*

NOTE:

Shrub roses and lilac underplanted with *Pulmonaria angustifolia*.

and fresh-looking blue-green leaves make this big perennial a beautiful foil for other flowers. The leathery dark green leaves of false dittany (*Dictamnus albus*), on a lower plane, are just as desirable. Of course, peony foliage is valued all spring and summer and into fall, when it starts to turn burnished tints.

Boltonia 'Snowbank' and Canadian burnet (*Sanguisorba canadensis*) are two late-blooming perennials with good foliage for the back borders of the garden. The *Boltonia* rises stiffly to four feet with linear glaucous leaves; the burnet makes tall graceful clumps of crimped pinnate leaves that remain a fresh green through the growing season.

Sedum 'Autumn Joy' flowers in September and October, but its compact clumps of fleshy light green leaves are of value all spring and summer. Chrysanthemums tend to have healthy foliage also, which is a good thing, for they too are a feature in the garden for many months before they bloom.

Siberian iris are appreciated for their arching grassy leaves, which stay healthier and better-looking than the swordlike leaves of their bearded cousins. Some of the hardy geraniums, or cranesbills, are a good choice for their beautiful, low mounding foliage. I particularly like to use *G. macrorrhizum* along a border's front edge for its bold, shapely leaves; they are a fine contrast to clumps of daylilies or Siberian iris. *G. sanguineum* and its pretty variety *striatum* are comely plants to edge a border and become attractively tinged with red as autumn approaches.

I like to include some well-behaved herbs among the perennials and shrubs in the flower borders to take advantage of their becoming greenery. Southernwood (*Artemisia abrotanum*) is always effective to soften a planting scheme with a haze of feathery pale green. Rue, with its curiously cut blue-green foliage and tidy habit, makes a superior ground cover for leggy roses and bold-leaved perennials (five plants together create a good show), remaining fresh-looking until frost. Fernleaf tansy, *Tanacetum vulgare* 'Crispum', with rich green crinkled leaves, is a grand filler for the back of the border. Sage (*Salvia officinalis*) in its dwarf form or in its handsome purple or golden-variegated dress is excellent as an edging among flowers and stays in good condition until winter.

A few small shrubs with pleasing foliage mixed into the flower border add substance to the picture. The dwarf Korean lilac is an exemplar, as is the bluebeard, *Caryopteris* × *clandonensis*, although this silver-leaved shrub is marginally hardy for me and is sometimes lost in a severe winter.

The shrubby potentillas (*P. fruticosa*) are worthwhile, having a good habit as well as profuse flowers. I like them billowing near the front of a border.

Rugosa roses can be added to the list of useful shrubs, and *Rosa glauca* with its unique plum-colored foliage. Some of the barberries can be used effectively among flowers. The dwarf red-leaved Japanese barberry is particularly appealing among clear pink and mauve-pink flowers.

The red-stemmed variegated dogwood, *Cornus alba* 'Elegantissima', is a small shrub with nicely marked leaves of green and creamy white. It will grow equally well in sun or semishade and is charming as a background for white and yellow flowers.

I could not end the list of good foliage without mentioning boxwood. The dwarf English box and Korean box (both hardy here in the coldest part of Zone 6) are never out of place in the flower garden with their rounded mounds of rich glossy green.

*

SUMMER
PHLOX

The phlox family is one of North America's most delightful contributions to the world of garden flowers. *Phlox subulata*, the best known of the rock garden varieties, and first to flower, clothes banks and stone walls with lively sheets of color (lavender, white, pink, and magenta) in April when forsythia is in bloom. *P. divaricata*, the spring phlox (also known as wild blue phlox), blooms later in May. It has soft lavender-blue flowers that rise a foot high from mat-forming leaves, sending waves of sweet fragrance into the air. It is lovely combined with tulips and late-flowering daffodils in the flower border, or planted in drifts with foamflower (*Tiarella cordifolia*) and ferns in the woodland garden. *P. sto-*

SUMMER PHLOX

lonifera, with blue or white flowers, is a similar kind though lower-growing and also makes an enchanting ground cover for the verges of a woodland path. *P. maculata* 'Miss Lingard' is an excellent variety for the flower border in early summer. It sends up two- to three-foot stems of slender leaves topped by elegant cylindrical heads of stark white flowers for several weeks starting in mid-June.

But the grandest member of the phlox family, the biggest and splashiest and most merry, is summer phlox, *P. paniculata*. Like tulips in May, summer phlox brings a unique gaiety to the August garden. With great fragrant heads of white and pale pink, bright pink, cherry red, scarlet, and lavender, it puts on a dazzling show that continues for weeks; and if you are careful to snip off the blooms as they fade, summer phlox will hardly take a breath before flowering again on secondary stems, extending its radiant color well into September.

Summer phlox is not a particularly "easy-care" perennial in our climate. Although it will flower in either sun or light shade and rarely requires staking, it suffers in our spells of drought and needs regular deep drinks of water in order to bloom well. Furthermore, our ghastly summer heat and humidity often cause the leaves to mildew if the plants have not been sprayed periodically with a fungicide like Benlate. Its preference is for a rich soil (flourishing on generous applications of old manure from the barnyard), and it requires division and replanting every few years for the best display. I should mention, too, that, along with daylilies and hosta, summer phlox is at the top of the list of perennials the deer love to eat. Some unlucky years I have had the buds neatly nipped off all my plants each time they were about to bloom.

If you live in a deer-infested area like ours, some sort of preventive measure is required to enjoy the flowering of phlox. Nevertheless, despite its demands, I would not want to be without masses of this perennial in the garden. It is unbeatable for splashes of clear joyful color, and as a bonus, it throws off a haunting peppery fragrance into the summer air.

Early and late varieties of summer phlox (catalogs usually specify which are which) can be planted to take maximum advantage of the long season of bloom. 'Gaiety' and 'Starfire' are two early bloomers here, beginning to flower by mid-July. They are both brilliant in color, the former a shocking pink, the latter a vivid cherry red, that are stunning in combination with dull blues (the color of globe thistles and veronicas), creamy whites, and clear yellows.

'Dodo Hanbury Forbes' is a midseason favorite that is a clear medium pink. 'Fairest One' is another telling pink, soft and luminous. These are splendid varieties to plant in generous clumps with pink beebalm and pale yellow daylilies.

The white cultivars, like 'World Peace' and 'Mt. Fuji', are charming grown in shadowy parts of the garden with balloon flowers (*Platycodon grandiflorus*) and spires of blue lobelia. In a sunnier border, white phlox combine well with the gaudy golden daisies of heliopsis and rudbeckias and the fuzzy spikes of purple liatris.

Older gardens are often full of self-seeded clumps of old-fashioned summer phlox in soft hues of blue-pink or magenta. These are invariably healthier and more robust than the hybrids we buy, and are pleasing to see in drifts by themselves, especially in shadowy places, or planted with flowers of complementary color like buttery yellow evening primroses and mulleins, soft blue veronicas and *Perovskia*, or the tall cream panicles of *Artemisia lactiflora*. They make an effective picture, too, with other flowers of coloring similar to their own, like the musk mallows, Joe-Pye weed, and purple loosestrife. But it is best to keep them some distance from the hybrid summer phlox, many of which tend toward shades of warm pink. Planted together, the blue pinks and the warm pinks merely detract from each other.

RUDBECKIAS

It is heresy, I know, but I prefer the wild black-eyed Susan (*Rudbeckia hirta*) to the much-touted popular variety of rudbeckia called 'Goldsturm'. This is not to say that the wild black-eyed Susan is a better plant for the garden. It is not. It is a short-lived annual or biennial with foliage that succumbs to

BLACK-EYED SUSAN
(*Rudbeckia hirta*)

our humid weather and becomes ratty by August; *R.* 'Gold-sturm' (*R. fulgida sullivantii* 'Goldsturm' is its official name) is a hardy perennial with dark green leaves that stay healthy all summer despite humidity and searing heat. And, because 'Goldsturm' is compact in habit and exceedingly floriferous, it creates mounds of golden color in the garden.

But this popular cultivar has none of the grace of the native black-eyed Susan. The flowers of 'Goldsturm' are stiff and large, the stems unyielding, growing rather like pins in a pincushion. Our wild rudbeckia, on the other hand, has smaller, finer flowers that lean and sway on graceful stems.

Enjoying each of them for different reasons, I have both varieties of rudbeckia in my nasturtium border. The black-eyed Susan, with its golden rays and appealing chocolate-brown disk, rises from basal clumps of gray-green ovate leaves and begins to bloom in early July, a few weeks before 'Goldsturm'. Although a short-lived plant, it will seed itself in the garden, and I let it mingle with its more stalwart cousin. In August I cut most of the flowering stems down to the ground before they become unsightly. Then I enjoy the health and vigor and splashy display of 'Goldsturm' for the rest of the month.

Once considered a rudbeckia, the purple coneflower is now listed as *Echinacea purpurea*. It is a coarse-leaved plant about three feet high with marvelous large daisylike flowers of rose pink, the rays surrounding a prominent boss of warm reddish brown. This is a showy flower for the sunny border in July and August, nice combined with yellow daylilies and the shaggy heads of pink beebalm and clumps of bright pink phlox. A striking white variety called 'White Swan' is somewhat lower-growing, with a whirl of petals surrounding a central cone-shaped disk of copper and green. These cone-flowers have a curious look as they expand from bud to flower. At first their rays are spiky and upright, but gradually they elongate and spread out, becoming reflexed in full bloom.

All the rudbeckias and coneflowers are striking in bouquets because of their combination of brilliant color and prominent black (or brown) eyes. For cutting, I much prefer the graceful wild black-eyed Susan to the stiff short-stemmed 'Goldsturm', but this cultivar is cheerful too in small jugs with French marigolds and feverfew, nasturtiums, and sprigs of sage.

When tidying the garden for winter, consider not cutting these flowers down. The stark stems carry their dark cones through the winter months and are picturesque against a blanket of snow.

❦

NESTING
DUCK

One of the Pekin ducks has made a nest in a stand of tansy in the herb garden. She is virtually hidden from sight among the tall green fronds, and I think it must be a pleasant place to spend her day, shaded from the summer sun and enjoying whiffs of fernlike scent from the tansy leaves above her. If I come too close along the gravel path, she hisses softly. At dusk she covers her nest carefully with dried fronds and feathers and goes up to the barnyard for a swim.

By nightfall she has retired with the other ducks and chick-

ens to the safety of the henhouse. Eventually, when she feels she has laid enough eggs, she will want to sit on her nest through the night. But I will gather up the eggs at that point, for if I let her set she would surely be killed by a nocturnal raccoon or fox out on a prowl, who would catch wind of her nestled in the tansy unprotected.

THE
NASTURTIUM
BORDER

The nasturtium border started life as an extension of the vegetable garden, a place where I could grow the gaudy flowers of summer, the golden yellow and orange and scarlet ones that I love to cut for bouquets. I am expanding it now to make a double border, through which we will walk on our way from the kitchen to the barn.

The beds will be backed by white and yellow flowering shrubs — the early *Abeliophyllum* and winter honeysuckle, the rugosa roses 'Agnes' and *alba*, the small *Viburnum opulus* 'Compactum', and one of the fragrant mock oranges.

I am tucking dozens of early golden yellow and cream-colored crocuses among the shrubs for puddles of color to cheer us in March. Patches of small daffodils will continue the color into April, and sprightly violas (the apricot 'Chantrey-land' and rich brown 'Arkwright Ruby') will flower among the burgeoning perennials. I am planting a dwarf bearded iris of soft peach color to mingle with the bright orange buttercup flowers of geum and the little yellow-and-red-striped *Tulipa chrysantha* in May.

Here I will have fiery red Oriental poppies to flaunt their glorious color in June when the viburnum is laced with white disks of flowers. 'Agnes' will open its soft yellow crumpled blooms behind single-flowering white peonies.

I will allow the yellow loosestrife, *Lysimachia punctata*, to spread in good drifts in the middle of the borders, for this showy perennial remains in bloom for many weeks in early summer. It is often described as invasive, but I do not find it troublesome; any excess is easily pulled up. It requires no staking and is unbothered by pests or diseases, and its hand-

NASTURTIUMS

some spires of rich yellow starry flowers create a lively display.

July in the nasturtium border will feature gold and apricot and orange daylilies, all those hues that I ban from the main garden, with its predominant clear pink coloring. Nasturtiums and calendulas will be inserted among clumps of purple sage and geums and dwarf iris for more of this cheerful color.

By high summer the daisy-flowering perennials take over the show. The brassy *Heliopsis helianthoides scabra* and black-eyed Susans will paint the borders lavishly with gold. (I will add some *Artemisia lactiflora*, whose tall creamy panicles will rest the eye from the pervading gaudiness.) Tall-growing heleniums carry the warm color into fall with their clusters of small crimped daisies in rich copper or in yellow.

By then the clustered fruit of the viburnum will have colored a soft red, and the rugosa roses will be littered with tomatolike hips. Some old-fashioned late-blooming chrysanthemums will supply the last patches of sunny color in the garden, lasting until hard frost.

❧

GERMANDER

Germander (*Teucrium chamaedrys*) is blooming in the herb garden, graceful spikes of mauve pink. This is an outstanding perennial that I think is too little known. Shrublike, low and compact, with small glossy leaves that are attractive all summer, it makes a first-rate edging for a garden border. By August it has billowed neatly over the border's edge and is a haze of purply pink spires that are effective for many weeks.

GERMANDER
(*Teucrium chamaedrys*)

Although it is semievergreen in warmer climates, germander is marginally hardy in New England, and even here it is slow to come alive in the spring. But by mid-May the bushes are rich and plump, with shiny dark green serrated leaves. Old plants that are very woody fare less well through the winter than young bushes; the centers tend to die out after a number of years. But germander can be easily propagated by layering (pin down a lax stem and cover it at this point with soil) or by rooting cuttings, and it even seeds itself in the gravel here in the herb garden.

If you are willing to forfeit the late-summer flowers, germander clips well and makes an excellent small geometric hedge. It is a favorite for making knot gardens. Here at Duck Hill I use it as a hedge in the vegetable garden, and it makes a delightful frame for the lettuces, beans, marigolds, and radishes in the two center beds. I clip the bushes hard once in the spring and once or twice in midsummer, keeping the height of the hedge at about ten inches.

Plant germander in full sun in a light rich soil; for a border or hedge, space the plants about nine inches apart. This southern European herb is unbothered by diseases or pests. It never requires staking, and except for a hard cutting back in April, if you are growing it naturally it needs no further attention. The long-lasting rosy flowers have a delicacy that keeps them from clashing with the bolder golds of the season, and they are charming cut for small mixed posies.

Germander has a sweet woodsy fragrance that is not thrown on the air but becomes apparent when the leaves are bruised.

SHRUBS
IN
BLOOM

Some delicately pretty shrubs bloom in August and September, when we hardly expect such pleasant offerings. In early August the sweet pepperbush, or summersweet, *Clethra alnifolia*, is covered with fragrant bottlebrush blooms in white or palest pink. This is a charming medium-sized shrub to use at the edge of the garden or in light woodland. (I have seen it, too, beautifully used grouped with evergreens to frame a swimming pool.) It has handsome ribbed simple leaves, a pleasing upright habit, and clusters of sweet-smelling flower spikes that last in bloom for several weeks. Several bushes of the variety 'Rosea' border the herb garden here at Duck Hill.

SWEET PEPPERBUSH
(*Clethra alnifolia*)

The pretty racemes are pink in bud, expanding into pale pink fuzz, and are invariably humming with bees. By the woodland path I have planted a few bushes of the more common white variety. This shrub is native to our eastern states, growing naturally in low damp woods. I have seen vast stretches of it lighting up boggy woodland in August with its frothy spires.

A small shrub blooming later in August that I recommend highly for inclusion in the flower border is *Caryopteris* × *clandonensis*, commonly known as bluebeard. It makes a tidy bush with simple silvery mint-scented leaves, a lovely foil of foliage in the garden all spring and summer. Then in late summer it starts to bloom, whorls of soft blue flowers (almost a true blue) held gracefully on wandlike branches. *Caryopteris* continues to bloom right through September, and even after the flowers stalks fade, they remain decorative. In winter the tiers of seed heads turn a creamy beige and, against a canvas of white and gray, seem almost to be blooming again. In our climate, bluebeard sometimes dies back over the winter, and I prune the branches back hard in the spring to encourage new growth from the base.

Perovskia atriplicifolia, or Russian sage, is somewhere between a shrub and a herbaceous perennial. When young, this herb is green and soft to the base; with age it gets woody and shrublike. It is another delicate blue-flowering, silver-leaved plant — so welcome in the heaviness of late summer. Pale lavender-blue spikes rise in a willowy fashion above lacy gray-green foliage; in full flower by the end of July and through August, it appears from a distance like a mist of blue. *Perovskia* is best planted in quantity (five or more plants) for good effect and may need a little twiggy support, for it tends to sprawl a bit. Mixed with lime-green nicotiana, purple sage, and catmint, it makes a satisfying picture in the herb garden. Like *Caryopteris*, Russian sage is best cut back hard in early spring.

Two treasured spring-flowering shrubs rebloom in August, a surprise bonus. The daphne lilac (*Syringa microphylla* 'Superba') once again throws off fragrant panicles of palest pink flowers that open from deep rose-pink buds. And *Daphne caucasica* is covered again in clusters of four-petaled white stars. Again I can bury my nose in the little flowers to inhale their heavenly fragrance.

There are two common shrubs flowering now that I do not have growing at Duck Hill but admire in the neighborhood. *Hydrangea paniculata* is a fountain of white plumes that will soon be tinged with pink. I always associate this shrub with tall Victorian houses, and certainly a vase of the great plumes, pinkish beige by winter, is a typical decoration of that era. Nearby is a handsome hedge of this hydrangea several hundred feet long, and in bloom it makes an extravagant show. It is a shrub best suited to a big scale, I think.

The other ubiquitous August-flowering shrub in this area is rose-of-Sharon (*Hibiscus syriacus*). This is an awkward-looking shrub when not in leaf, and, unfortunately, it is so slow to leaf out in the spring that its rather ugly, stiff shape is then sorely apparent. But now, in late summer, the rose-of-Sharon comes into its own with exotic tropical-looking hibiscus flowers of white and pink and purple. I find the white-flowering ones, with their striking maroon centers particularly appealing; used as a flowering hedge or mixed with other shrubs, they are an engaging sight for several weeks.

CALENDULAS

✧

ANNUALS

I don't have anywhere near as much room for annuals as I would like. How satisfying they are now, and how much I appreciate their gaudy flowery faces in the late-summer garden. How fine they look, too, in our New England villages planted in island beds and tubs and window boxes, an indiscriminate riot of color, an explosion of exuberance and merriment.

It is now, in August, that I turn with modest pleasure to our small vegetable garden, where I have sown various ordinary kinds of annuals for some splashy Mexican color. Zinnias are here in their clear tones of golden yellow and scarlet and pink, and in their curious striped dress (so coveted by Vita Sackville-West that she had an American friend send her seeds yearly). The fiery 'Diablo' and 'Sunset' varieties of cosmos, fine small flowers with zing, are tucked in the beds. Calendulas are included if I think to sow them early in the spring, for I love these frank and cheerful old-time marigolds. I plant sunflowers here too for late-summer cutting — not the giant ones we usually associate with vegetable gardens, but the small-flowering kinds like 'Italian White' and 'Picolo'. These make four-foot plants with flowers about four inches in diameter, long-stemmed and dramatic with their central boss of black, wonderfully striking in large bouquets.

All sorts of useful annuals can be added to the mixed border or perennial garden for a dash of color lasting from now until frost. The tall-growing cosmos in white or mauve pink is effective in the background of the garden among plants with more substantial foliage. Cleome, the spider plant, is equally pleasant planted in good blocks or drifts. I always try to grow from seed or buy a few flats of *Salvia farinacea* to sprinkle in among the perennials. This rather insignificant-looking plant throws up slender spikes of deep purple-blue flowers in late summer that are a delightful addition to a border. 'Blue Bedder' is the best variety, being fairly tall (to three feet). 'Victoria' is a more compact sort for planting near the front of the border.

In shadowy places in the garden, nothing is more effective than stands of the tall fragrant white-flowering *Nicotiana alata*. Fortunately, once you have planted it, you can count on seedlings to appear each summer (if you are not too meticulous a weeder), and these can be readily transplanted to the spots where you want them to grow. The 'Nicki' hybrids in pink and rose and white are dwarf in stature, nice near the front of the border but, unfortunately, without the wonderful nighttime fragrance.

I always include some white and blue petunias for their delicious scent (these colors seem to smell the best), either in pots or tucked around low-growing perennials in the garden.

Sky-blue *Nigella damascena*, or love-in-a-mist, seeds itself around the sundial in the herb garden, the descendants of a packet of seeds (the variety 'Miss Jekyll') given to me by a friend years ago. This is a whimsical flower with delicate wheels of blue above finely cut foliage, and curious balloon-like seed heads. Louise Beebe Wilder calls it "the bluest and the quaintest, the most old fashioned and the prettiest" of blue annuals.

Borage echoes the color in its starlike flowers, beloved by bees. Dill is here too, with its Scandinavian-scented leaves and lacy wheels of chartreuse flowers that are a charming light touch in bouquets. I often plant purple heliotrope among the herbs for its vibrant color and vanillalike fragrance.

Many of the more unusual tender sages are tempting to grow for their dramatic late-summer and early-fall spikes of color. But here a frosty night often strikes them down just as they are coming into flower. I grow pineapple sage (*Salvia elegans*) anyway for its fruity-smelling leaves (they really do smell of pineapple), and in a mild autumn I enjoy the vivid scarlet racemes of flowers. *Salvia leucantha* is another tender sage worth growing for its tall, boldly striking foliage. If we are blessed with mellow weather in late September, it throws up great spikes of lavender and purple. This year I have planted *Salvia uliginosa* in a blank spot in the herb garden. What an unfortunate name for a sage that has graceful spikes of sky-blue flowers at the end of summer. These unfamiliar sages are often available in pots at local herb nurseries, and it is fun at the last minute to sneak a new sort of annual into the summer garden.

🎋

MEADOW
FLOWERS

PURPLE LOOSESTRIFE
(*Lythrum salicaria*)

The low fields around Duck Hill are ablaze with purple flowers. That notorious colonizer from Europe, purple loosestrife (*Lythrum salicaria*), is in glorious bloom. Its spires of radiant magenta punctuate the verges of the ponds and rise in bold clumps from the swampy meadows. Our native vervain (*Verbena hastata*) is here too, pencil-thin spikes of deep violet blue, often accompanied by drowsing bees. Joe-Pye weed (*Eupatorium purpureum*) softens the picture with great puffs of dusty mauve rising often six feet high above stout leaves and stems. Deepest in color, the tall ironweed (*Vernonia noveboracensis*) opens its clusters of rich purple. At a distance, ironweed may be mistaken for an aster, but on closer inspection it reveals clusters of thistlelike blooms.

Nature lightens this summer scene of purple hues with a dusting of Queen Anne's lace, still in bloom, and great clumps of Japanese knotweed (*Polygonum cuspidatum*), dripping now with creamy white flowers on its arching branches. Sweeps of goldenrod are in green-yellow bud, waiting to take the stage in September, when their graceful sunlit sprays are in full flower.

❦

ALLIUMS

It is time to think about ordering some alliums from the bulb catalogs. Each year I try to add one or two new varieties to my shopping list, for the ornamental onions are a beguiling family of plants. Without taking up much space at all, they add a punch to the garden borders, like upside-down exclamation points, and many of them are strikingly colorful. Most of the alliums have foliage that yellows and disappears soon after blooming (chives, broad-leaved chives, and curly chives are valuable exceptions), and therefore it is important to plant them (like tulips and daffodils) where good foliage of perennials and shrubs will mask their decomposition.

Allium aflatunense, the first to bloom at Duck Hill in early May, has large balls of intense red-violet starlike flowers on slender thirty-inch stems. It lasts in bloom for several weeks, in fact for most of May, and is splendid to see in the herb garden behind clouds of yellow-green lady's mantle flowering at the same time. The broad basal leaves of this allium begin to yellow even as it is flowering, so it is best to conceal the base of the plants with a foreground planting of good foliage. I have interwoven the bulbs with clumps of *Achillea* 'Coronation Gold', and the yarrow's soft feathery green leaves help to camouflage the alliums as they fade. There is a white variety of *A. aflatunense* that I covet, having seen it in a friend's garden, where the perfect white globes made a wonderful

Allium moly

picture rising above impeccably trimmed boxwood hedging that framed the narrow flower beds.

A. oreophilum is a much less dramatic sort that also blooms in May. Rising to a mere six inches, this allium is more suited to the rock garden or for intimate viewing. It has loose umbels of rosy pink stars held upright above narrow straplike leaves. Scattered through a front border of golden lemon thyme in the herb garden, this little allium puts on a brief but pretty show. By June it has disappeared, and the clumps of thyme have filled in where it bloomed.

Allium moly has a similar habit, although it is stouter in leaf and taller in flower (to about one foot), and the upright clusters of starry flowers are a bright clear yellow. Blooming in early June, this is a cheerful plant to scatter around a rose bush (here, in the herb garden, it makes a becoming ground cover for the striped pink-and-white *Rosa mundi*), or to wind in among front-border perennials in a yellow and white garden (as I have seen it used in England).

Surely chives (*A. schoenoprasum*) is the best known of the alliums, prized as a flavoring in sauces, soups, and salads. But how fine it looks in the flower border or herb garden in June when its mauvy lavender tufts are in bloom! The gray-green grasslike clumps mingle pleasantly here with foxgloves and apple mint and bright yellow yarrow.

The most striking allium in the June garden is star of Persia, *A. christophii*. Rising fifteen inches high, the flower is a perfect ball of spiky stars about eight inches in diameter. This bizarre globe is a soft silvery lavender, and it has an airy quality that keeps it from seeming top-heavy. The silvery balls scattered around the deeper purple spires of *Salvia superba* make a handsome picture. By the end of June, the flower color has faded; the balls become dry and light tan in color, but because of their extraordinary pattern, they remain an attractive feature in the garden.

Taller, its large globe more densely packed with lilac flowers, *A. giganteum* makes quite a punch in the garden in June. At three feet, it is the tallest of the alliums and can be used with great effect toward the back of a flower border, where it contrasts nicely with the early lemon daylilies and pink and white roses.

All of these spherical alliums are prized by dried flower arrangers, for even after the heads have faded, they hold their unique structure and are striking in winter bouquets.

The drumstick allium (*A. sphaerocephalum*) is a likable oddity in the July garden. Waving atop slender two- to three-foot stems, the nubby oval heads are rich red violet. They are not large, perhaps the size of a tablespoon, and have a peppery effect in the garden. They are wonderful planted in generous patches (fifty bulbs together are not too many) among pale yellow flowers, such as *Coreopsis* 'Moonbeam' or one of the shrubby potentillas. I have also seen drumstick alliums planted picturesquely with clumps of a variegated grass and pink-flowering veronica and the dwarf red-leaved barberry, which echoes their hue. This allium, along with *A. moly*, is relatively inexpensive, so it is tempting to plant it with abandon.

A. cernuum is flowering by the middle of July, small explosions of soft lavender-pink flowers from pale drooping buds. This native American is a quietly pretty allium for the middle of the border, a nice foil for some of the stronger-colored flowers of summer. Its grasslike foliage does not disappear after flowering but remains green, like chives, throughout the growing season.

The best allium for lasting foliage — in fact the only allium I know of that has distinctly effective foliage in the garden — is broad-leaved chives, *A. senescens*. This ornamental onion grows in stout clumps of straplike leaves that are a handsome contrast in the herb garden to mounds of wild marjoram, golden-variegated sage, and fernleaf tansy. In late July and August, broad-leaved chives throw up sturdy two- to three-foot stems topped by lovely heads of starry lavender flowers that last several weeks in bloom.

A dwarf variety of *A. senescens* called *glaucum*, or curly chives, is of equal value. It also has lasting and effective foliage, but in this case the leaves grow in low swirling clumps that are ideal as an edging to a border. In late July buds appear above the mounds of glaucous leaves and by mid-August are in bloom, miniature lavender spheres.

Garlic chives, *A. tuberosum*, is the last allium to bloom in my garden. Above rather messy grasslike foliage that I have been muttering about all summer suddenly appear beautiful heads of starry white flowers that more than make up for the disheveled look of the leaves. I love to cut this elegant allium for bouquets. Indeed, all the alliums are marvelous for adding a zest or punch to flower arrangements, just as they do in the garden.

September

FEVERFEW
(*Chrysanthemum parthenium*)

Just as some plants are useful in flower arrangements as fillers — that is, to fill in the bouquet and create a backdrop for more striking flowers — so there are plants in the garden that I consider useful in a similar way, for filling in the spaces around other, more assertive perennials and shrubs. Subtly, without fanfare, they bind the picture together with their flowers or their foliage.

Feverfew (*Chrysanthemum parthenium*) is one of these plants that fills the voids, in this case with billows of tiny cream-white daisies above ferny foliage. This lighthearted daisy is a short-lived perennial, but it seeds itself with abandon in my garden, and I let it fill in around the stouter perennials and shrubs mid-border in the garden beds. It is an undemanding flower, thriving in either sun or dappled shade, and can be had in double or single form, both of which I find decorative. Excess plants are easily pulled up any time of year, so its habit of seeding about never becomes troublesome.

Baby's breath (*Gypsophila paniculata*) has the same sort of effectiveness in the flower border. This old-fashioned plant unfortunately does not thrive at Duck Hill, I suspect because where I have it planted — in the white garden — it does not get quite enough sun. If it will flourish in your garden (give it a sweet soil, good drainage, and full sun), it creates a wonderful foil in bloom for the bolder flowers of early summer. It is useful, too, as Gertrude Jekyll points out, for masking the disappearance of splashy early-blooming Oriental poppies, which yellow and die down after flowering.

In September and October, *Boltonia asteroides* serves as a foil at the back of the borders with clouds of white asterlike daisies above glaucous leaves. Sometimes the panicled aster (*Aster simplex*) sneaks into the garden beds from its more natural habitat at the wood's edge and in nearby thickets, and if it were not so rampant, there would be little to complain about this wild plant as a filler in the flower border. It is similar in looks to the boltonia, except for the smaller size of its many flowers and the dark green of its leaves. As the flower heads mature, the rays are often tinted blue.

For foliage in half-shaded places, nothing is more attractive as a filler than sweet cicely (*Myrrhis odorata*). This licorice-scented herb has lacy fernlike leaves that spread in a horizontal manner and make a graceful skirt for leggy perennials and shrubs. The delicate umbels of white flowers (not unlike Queen Anne's lace) are an added bonus in May. Sweet cicely seeds itself where the situation suits it, and the young plants can be moved in early spring to your design. With age, the plants develop a fleshy taproot and are more difficult to transplant.

Fernleaf tansy (*Tanacetum vulgare* 'Crispum') is a favorite of mine for the back of the border among the tall shrub roses.

FERNLEAF TANSY
(*Tanacetum vulgare* 'CRISPUM')

Its rich green crinkled leaves are as valuable in the garden as they are when used as a background in bouquets. Its flowers are insignificant — little gold buttons produced in small clusters in midsummer — and I ignore them. This is a plant to use for its splendid foliage. If the summer weather is excessive (is it ever not?), tansy sometimes loses its lowest leaves, but this failing can be masked by medium-sized perennials planted in front of it.

Southernwood (*Artemisia abrotanum*) and rue are two other herbs I rely on as fillers. The artemisia adds a soft feathery texture wherever it is used. I find it particularly useful in sunny borders for planting among roses; the bushy southernwood effectively hides their legginess and contrasts nicely with their bolder leaves and showier flowers. Rue (*Ruta graveolens*), with its low clumps of elegantly cut blue-green foliage, can be lavished on empty spaces in the garden like a ground cover.

In a damp, half-shaded bed of the main garden, lemon balm (*Melissa officinalis*) weaves around the daylilies and beebalms and fills in where the old-fashioned bleeding heart is fading. This sweet-smelling member of the mint family has a bushy habit, fresh green ovate leaves, and small cream-colored flowers in tiers.

Many of the tender scented geraniums are good fillers in the summer garden. After the danger of frost has passed, I like to add them to the herb garden beds, where their decorative leaves will spread around the more substantial herbs. They are also useful for planting in big outdoor pots and window boxes either by themselves or around splashy blooming annuals.

In the woodland garden, nothing is more valuable as a filler than ferns, which carpet the ground under shrubs and deciduous trees where, in early spring, there were masses of bulbs.

ON

MEADOWS

Driving through the New England countryside, I am struck by the artistry of the natural meadows that are so much a part of our scenery. Creating meadows at home is very popular now, with the desire for informal, less laborious gardening, and I think we can learn a great deal from studying, and copying as best we can, the makeup of nature's meadows around us.

I am suspicious of the "meadows in a can" that you see for

sale in hardware stores and catalogs. Too often they are full of flowers native to other parts of the United States and Europe, which, even if they survive our climate, look unnatural here. If you are creating a meadow — and nothing could be more pleasant as a substitute for extensive lawns — I think it is important to stick mostly to those flowers that are indigenous to your area. In the Northeast, they would include oxeye daisies and buttercups, ragged robin and Queen Anne's lace, yarrow and black-eyed Susans, butterfly weed, goldenrod, and asters. If you are patient, these meadow flowers will gradually appear on their own accord in a field that is mowed once a year, in the fall. To hurry the process along, you can transplant clumps of flowers from an established meadow and then let them go to seed, or scatter seed that you have gathered or bought.

The main ingredient of your meadow, however, the canvas upon which your flowers are painted, is, ideally, wild grasses. If you look at meadows in the countryside, you will notice that the most pleasing consist primarily of soft waving grasses

GOLDENROD

(in themselves a lovely sight) through which are painted spatterings of flower color. There are exceptions; vast solid stretches of purple loosestrife are a common sight in wet fields and along waterways, and goldenrod can colonize closely enough to seem to exclude all other plants. But generally, the main theme of the meadow, the serene backdrop that sets off and complements the drifts of seasonal flowers, is the soft green and beige of grasses. Meadow flowers are ethereal, a stunning sight one week, gone to seed the next; but the grasses remain beautiful throughout the seasons.

Be sure to mow a wide path through your meadow for walking. Few things are more alluring than a closely mowed path curving out of sight in a field of high grasses and flowers.

❧

LATE-BLOOMING
DAYLILY

I have an unusual daylily blooming now, a hybrid called 'Autumn Prince'. The last daylily to bloom in my garden, it is also the tallest-growing and has the smallest flowers.

What charming flowers they are, simple trumpets, no more than three inches across, of pale golden yellow deepening at the throat. Like some of the old-fashioned varieties of daylilies, the flowers have a light sweet fragrance. They are borne in clusters above waving five-foot stems and open continuously through August and September.

'Autumn Prince' is the most delicate daylily I know, more delicate even than the early species that charm me with their simplicity and fragrance in early June. Because of its height, it looks well at the back of the border, but with its good daylily foliage and graceful habit, it could stand alone or mingle with lower perennials midborder.

In the main garden it blooms cheerfully in the shade of one of the crabapples and makes a fine picture with the greenish white bottlebrush blooms of Canadian burnet, clumps of white summer phlox, and, in the foreground, *Sedum* 'Autumn Joy', at first in green bud, then gradually turning from dusty pink to deep rose.

I have earmarked a clump of 'Autumn Prince' to be moved to the back reaches of the nasturtium border, where it will consort agreeably with the tall yellow heleniums blooming there at the same time. The color of the daylily is similar

DAYLILY 'AUTUMN PRINCE'

to that of the helenium, and its trumpet flowers will be a welcome contrast to the masses of small fringed daisies.

꘍

SIGNS
OF
AUTUMN

Our gander honks and flaps his wings in what seems like a gesture of comradeship as the Canada geese fly noisily overhead, practicing now for their trip south. Does the sound and sight of those wild geese stir in our domestic pair a deep instinctive urge to migrate? Like most domestic fowl (ducks and chickens as well as geese), they are too heavy to be airborne, although they often try, using the barn road as their runway. Starting at one end, they hurtle along, one in front of the other, flapping their wings wildly in a cloud of dust. As they gain speed along the last stretch of road, they often lift and glide for a moment, skimming the ground, then land with a racket of honking. Obviously satisfied with this feat of exercise, they resume their dignified parading and poking for bugs around the barnyard.

The swamp maples are flushed now with red. Virginia creeper, already in its crimson garb, climbs stone walls and decaying trees by the roadside, and viburnums and dogwoods are laden with fruit, as is our native winterberry.

With the cooler air and gentler sun, there is a new surge of growth in the garden. Catmint flowers again, roses offer pink-tinged blooms for vases and lapels, seedlings of foxgloves and feverfew and lungwort grow lustily in the borders.

Chrysanthemums, scorned in other seasons, are welcomed now as they expand into bloom, adding splashes of lovely autumnal color to the garden. On tall willowy stems, Japanese anemones open their exquisite flowers, like Fabergé jewels in silky white and mauve pink.

Colchicums, the naked ladies of autumn, suddenly appear beneath trees and shrubs. Without warning, they seem to spring from the earth, great goblets of lavender and slender chalices of white, in their freshness an astonishing sight as the days mellow and the leaves of the trees begin to fall.

❧

WINGED EUONYMUS

The winged euonymus bushes that grace the roadside and grow wild at the edge of the woods are tinged with red, another sign of autumn's arrival. *Euonymus alata* is not a native of America but was introduced from Asia more than a

WINGED EUONYMUS
(*Euonymus alata*)

century ago and has become naturalized widely in our area.

There is no season when I do not admire this fine shrub. In winter I am struck by its graceful shape and intriguing corky branches that interlace and sweep the ground in a rather Oriental fashion. In early spring it is dressed in delicate leaves of the freshest green. All summer it presents an agreeable picture, clothing hillsides and roadways with its rounded spreading form. And then in autumn, the foliage of the winged euonymus gradually turns from rich green to a stunning rosy scarlet. The branches drip with crimson fruit, partially hidden beneath the leaves. Even in late fall, after the leaves have fallen, the bushes are often tinted with color from the rust-orange seed capsules that persist on the branches.

Winged euonymus takes clipping beautifully and is often used for hedges. For this purpose the dwarf variety 'Compactus' is usually recommended, although the name is misleading, for it naturally matures at about ten feet in height. However, with a minimum of clipping, it can be kept much lower than that, and the rounded form and healthy, attractive foliage create a superior hedge. My only complaint about 'Compactus' (and it is really quibbling) is that its autumn color — what I call a shocking pink — at its peak is almost screaming in its intensity. In a naturalistic setting, I prefer the regular winged euonymous, larger in leaf and taller-growing, its reddish pink fall coloring not quite so brilliant.

This past spring I planted small specimens of the dwarf variety, purchased from a mail-order nursery, to form the hedge around our new courtyard. I am impatient now to see the bushes grow, but eventually I will be grateful that the winged euonymus is a slow grower, for it will not require the maintenance of deciduous hedges like privet and barberry.

For now I must be content with how it looks in my mind's eye, four or five feet tall, dense and lush, creating a lovely private entrance to the house.

⁊

IN

DEFENSE

OF A

LAWN

There seem to be a lot of scornful essays in newspapers and magazines and books these days about our preoccupation with lawns, saying how silly it is, what a waste of energy. Inert surfaces are recommended instead — gravel, brick, or stone — or we are advised to turn the lawn into a low-maintenance flower-filled meadow.

But perhaps these critics are overlooking a few points in their eagerness to have us renounce our lawns. First of all, nothing sets off a flower garden quite like a trim green expanse of lawn in front of it. I think it doesn't have to be a perfect turf (mine is full of clover as well as less desirable interlopers like ground ivy). If it is mowed once a week and the edges kept trim, even an imperfect lawn is a handsome complement to flowers and foliage shapes in the garden beds.

Of course there is labor in keeping lawns, even indifferent ones like mine. But it is wrong to think that inanimate surfaces are positively carefree (short of concrete and layers of black plastic). My gravel areas take a good deal of weeding and raking to look presentable. Gravel seems to be an ideal surface for the propagation of countless plants, some of them delightful additions, others decidedly not. Brick paving also needs periodic attention. All sorts of weeds love to sow between the cracks of the bricks, and pulling them up often dislodges the bricks. Of course, weed killer can be used (I occasionally resort to Roundup), but surely the less poison that sinks into our earth the better.

Furthermore, I think that many of these lawn detractors, when they carry on about the needless hours of labor a turf requires, forget that some people enjoy the activity of the weekly mowing. We have a neighbor whose wife kiddingly accuses him of hopping on his tractor mower every time his in-laws come to visit. Another neighbor, who spends his weekends here unwinding from a busy urban life, confessed to me recently that he was never happier than when out mowing, away from phones and pressing problems, alone with his thoughts, with the good smells of the country around him and the fine results of his effort instantly realized behind him.

Finally, is anything more pleasurable than flopping down on a lawn for a few minutes' rest on a pleasantly sunny day to pat the dog or chat with a visiting friend or child?

The only real stretch of lawn at Duck Hill is the square within the main garden. Occasionally the thought passes through my head that I might dig up this lawn and add four more garden beds (what madness!). But then I think how I would miss this serene patch of green. It is a perfect place for lounging with a dog or two by my side and surveying the results of my efforts in the garden.

I think the dogs would say a word or two, if they could, in favor of a lawn. I love to watch them as they roll deliciously from side to side, bury their noses among the blades, then

stretch their back legs flat out to get the full effect of the cool grass on their stomachs. No dog is tempted to luxuriate in such a fashion on gravel or brick.

CANADIAN BURNET

Canadian burnet (*Sanguisorba canadensis*) is a quiet, unassuming perennial. Nevertheless, it has considerable merit and is cherished by those who know it, a sleeper in the garden world. It will never set the world on fire with its flowers; they are not showy or colorful. Its foliage, although attractive all spring and summer, rarely elicits comment. But now, in September, when Canadian burnet blooms in the flower border or is cut for bouquets, it succeeds in gaining our attention and admiration, for its soft spires have the knack of enhancing all the flowers and foliage around it.

In a season replete with the round flowers of phlox and swirls of daisies, the curious bottlebrush blooms of Canadian burnet are a welcome relief. They develop quietly in August, at first nubby pencillike spikes on slender three- to four-foot stems, rising above arching clumps of narrow saw-toothed

Malus 'Katherine'

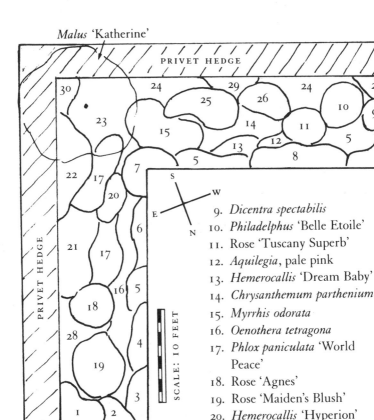

9. *Dicentra spectabilis*
10. *Philadelphus* 'Belle Etoile'
11. Rose 'Tuscany Superb'
12. *Aquilegia*, pale pink
13. *Hemerocallis* 'Dream Baby'
14. *Chrysanthemum parthenium*
15. *Myrrhis odorata*
16. *Oenothera tetragona*
17. *Phlox paniculata* 'World Peace'
18. Rose 'Agnes'
19. Rose 'Maiden's Blush'
20. *Hemerocallis* 'Hyperion'
21. *Sanguisorba canadensis*
22. *Iris sibirica* 'Caesar's Brother'
23. *Pulmonaria angustifolia*
24. *Digitalis purpurea*
25. *Rosa glauca*
26. *Aster novae-angliae* 'Alma Potschke'
27. *Melissa officinalis*
28. *Artemisia* 'Silver King'
29. *Mentha suaveolens*
30. *Hemerocallis* 'Autumn Prince'

SOUTHEAST BED OF MAIN GARDEN

1. *Hosta* 'Honeybells'
2. *Dicentra eximia*
3. *Iris pumila*, white
4. *Stachys byzantina*
5. *Astilbe* 'Peach Blossom'
6. *Sedum* 'Autumn Joy'
7. *Hosta* 'Thomas Hogg'
8. *Hosta fortunei marginata-alba*

NOTE:
Roses and mock orange underplanted with *Pulmonaria angustifolia*.

leaves. By the end of the month; the flowers begin to open from the bottom up into fuzzy, dense bottlebrushes, turning slowly from pale green to a dull soft white. Secondary flowers continue to develop through all of September, and it is this massed collection of spires that creates such a fine display at the back of the border.

Here at Duck Hill, in a shadowy bed of the main garden, Canadian burnet combines effectively with clumps of white phlox and *Artemisia* 'Silver King', bordered by a stretch of *Sedum* 'Autumn Joy' just turning pink. Another stand of burnet is in the herb garden, where it associates handsomely with fronds of fernleaf tansy and makes a fine backdrop of foliage all summer for clumps of broad-leaved chives and lady's mantle. The tall fuzzy blooms are a grand fall accent in this garden, and there are always plenty of small fresh spikes

CANADIAN BURNET
(*Sanguisorba canadensis*)

to cut for herbal posies. Combined with rue, sage, wild mar-joram, tansy, and Johnny-jump-ups, this intriguing flower always draws admiring comments.

Canadian burnet is a carefree perennial; it is untroubled by disease and does not require staking. Japanese beetles are said to enjoy its leaves, but in my garden they leave it alone, too busy, no doubt, eating roses. It will grow happily in sun or light shade and increases slowly over the years. I always find a small offshoot or two to give a gardening friend who has admired this subtle flower in my garden or in a bouquet. After years of unavailability in the trade (this is a plant handed on from one gardener to another), Canadian burnet is beginning to be offered by nurseries and mail-order catalogs.

There is a smaller burnet, a common denizen of culinary herb gardens that is better known. This is the salad burnet, *S. minor* (now more usually called *Poterium sanguisorba*), a

SALAD BURNET
Poterium sanguisorba

small, pretty plant with rosettes of delicate serrated leaflets that taste strongly of cucumber, and curious thimblelike flowers in early summer. It seeds about the garden in a pleasant way, and the young plants are particularly attractive. It is not a long-lived perennial — the plants seem to peter out after two or three years.

Another member of this family that I have just planted in the main garden (squeezed in would be a more accurate description), having discovered it in a local nursery, is *S. obtusa*, the Japanese burnet. It is said to have very decorative arching pink plumes on four-foot stems. The clumps of pinnate leaves are fresh and attractive even at this late season, so I have placed this new burnet at a side edge of one of the beds, where I could use some good foliage. I look forward to the large pink bottlebrushes next year.

❧

SOME
BERRIED
SHRUBS

Not only flowers decorate the garden in September. This is the month that begins the pageant of beautiful fruits. All summer they have been quietly developing, hips and drupes, pomes and berries, changing in color from dull soft browns and greens to brilliant red and orange, rose pink, frosted blue, white, and golden yellow. Some are fleeting in their glory, quickly eaten by our birds; others last weeks, sometimes months, coloring the late fall and early winter landscape.

Cotoneaster apiculatus, the cranberry cotoneaster, is one of the first shrubs here to be covered with fruit, beginning sometime in midsummer, and they persist well into winter. The berries are brilliant scarlet in color, the size of peas, and are dotted profusely along the recumbent branches of small dark green leaves. This attractive, low-growing cotoneaster drapes the stone walls on either side of the steps leading up from the terrace. Like many of the low, spreading varieties of cotoneaster, it is a pleasure to see in every season. In spring it is littered with tiny pink flowers, which will develop into the berries (actually pomes) of summer and fall. All summer the foliage remains glossy and dark green, turning maroon red by late autumn. In winter, when the leaves have fallen, the curious branching of the shrub becomes apparent, interlacing and hugging the stones in a graceful Oriental way.

Just above the terrace steps, in the nasturtium border, *Viburnum opulus* 'Compactum' is dressed now with clusters of glossy round fruit that is a soft red-orange in color. These will last about a month before the birds discover them and are lovely in a garden (or a bouquet) of tawny autumn colors.

There are numerous viburnums to grow for their fruit as well as those noted for their May flowers, and I hope eventually to have a collection of them growing along the barn road. (I am slowly hacking away at the weed trees and brambles presently flourishing in this area. How much I look forward to seeing handsome berried viburnums instead!) Three young bushes of *V. dilatatum* are established there already and are in fruit for the first time this year. This is a handsome upright viburnum, densely furnished with bold dark green leaves, roundly oval in shape, and with clusters of tiny teardrop drupes that turn gradually from green to bright scarlet. From a distance, the delicate clusters of fruit create a

Viburnum dilatatum

deep red haze against the dark foliage. The fruit is said to
persist long after the leaves (russet-colored in autumn) have
fallen. Plantsmen recommend planting several clones of
V. dilatatum together for the best display of berries.

I am still cosseting several young bushes of *V. cassinoides* in
the vegetable garden, but these will soon be moved to the barn
road. I await their fruiting with eagerness, for the display is
described as spectacular, the clusters of berries changing from
green to pink, then to blue and finally black. Known also for
its red autumn foliage and extreme hardiness, *V. cassinoides*,
or withe-rod, is a native of our northeastern United States.
A fairly small viburnum (about six feet in width and height),
it could easily be incorporated into an informal border of
flowers and shrubs. Several bushes massed together would
create the best effect.

Arrowwood (*V. dentatum*) was here when we came, tall
arching bushes of it growing happily enough in damp ground
beneath ash and maples. This is a handsome native shrub (I

doubt if there exists an unattractive viburnum) most suitable,
I think, to the wilder places of the garden. It has lustrous dark
green leaves, creamy white cymes of flowers in May, and
blue-black fruit that develops in September and is quickly
eaten by the birds. The leaves turn a purply red color before
falling in late October.

Growing alongside the arrowwood behind our barn in
great rounded clumps is the gray dogwood, *Cornus racemosa*.
It is bronze-leaved now and laden with chalky white berries
on rose-red stalks. Soon the fruit will be gone, eaten by the
birds, but the red fruit stalks, or pedicels, will remain, giving
the shrubs a pleasing rosy haze through winter. This native
shrub is marvelous for massing in semiwild places, either in
the sun or in the shade of high trees. It will spread into good-
sized colonies, and it can be sheared to keep the bushes dense
and compact. In early autumn bouquets, the bronze leaves
and white berries make a fine background for asters and
Japanese anemones.

By mid-September, the winterberry (*Ilex verticillata*) is
peppered with shiny Christmas-red berries, and these will
remain on the branches of this deciduous holly long after the
leaves have fallen. Winterberry is another of our native treasures, thriving in damp meadows and at the edge of the
woods all around us. It is a tall shrub in the wild, somewhere
between ten and twenty feet in height. In cultivation it is
rarely that tall, and dwarf cultivars of it are also available.
I like to see a grand sweep of winterberry at the fringes of the
garden; it is a stunning sight in late fall, studded with berries
so brilliant in the gray landscape they almost seem iridescent.
As with all hollies, a male plant is required nearby in order for
the female bushes to fruit. If I think of it, in late October or

early November I cut branches of winterberry and store them in pails of water in the barn, to be used later in holiday arrangements. By December there will be few berries left on the bushes outdoors, for the birds will have had their feast.

The common barberries have wonderfully decorative berries. Our naturalized barberry (*Berberis vulgaris*), which is so prevalent in fields and light woodland, and *B. thunbergii* have glossy scarlet fruit as bright as holly berries. These will persist through much of winter, and in fact are often still decorating the branches as they begin to leaf out in spring. The red-leaved Japanese barberry (*B. thunbergii atropurpurea*) is at its best now, with clusters of elegant slender oval fruit, a glistening rose red, that hang from the arching branches under wine-red leaves.

October

Helenium 'BUTTERPAT'

FLOWERS FOR A WEDDING BOUQUET

JAPANESE ANEMONES

A friend called me today (it is October 2) to ask if there was anything in my garden that she could pick to include in a bouquet for her son's wedding. Well, there are asters, of course, in many shades of lavender and purple and pink, but their flowers tend to close up at night and do not always last long in water.

The asterlike *Boltonia asteroides* 'Snowbank' could be used instead, for its flowers last well when cut for arrangements. This grand, fresh-looking perennial is in full bloom now and is a feature in the white garden. It is a tall-growing plant (to four feet) with a neat bushy habit and healthy gray-green leaves. Although the individual flowers are small and rather delicate-looking up close, they grow in masses, and the overall effect is of a large mound of soft white, which lightens the back of the border or a bouquet.

White and dusky pink Japanese anemones are at their peak and add a fragile elegance to any bouquet. I savor every day of their flowering, knowing they will be struck down by the first good frost of the month.

217

Most of the chrysanthemums are also in their prime — tall shaggy white ones tinged with pink in the white garden, mounds of pale rose ones in the main garden. A patch of burgundy button chrysanthemums in one of the borders exactly echoes the final coloring of that stellar sedum, 'Autumn Joy'.

For tall vertical accents, the Canadian burnet still offers fresh spikes of dull soft white. The last of the snakeroots, *Cimicifuga simplex*, is just starting to open its more delicate, lighter spires. The waving racemes of flowers do not grow as tall as those of the July-blooming black snakeroot (*C. racemosa*). But they are similar in looks, graceful narrow bottlebrushes, elegant in the garden or in a bouquet.

The old-fashioned white *Nicotiana* blooms on and on and is lovely and fragrant in flower arrangements. Although in the garden the waxy white flowers close up in the midday sun and do not open again until dusk, indoors they remain open day and night.

The rich purple spikes of *Salvia farinacea* and the sky-blue racemes of *S. uliginosa* could be added to these pink and white flowers to vary the bouquet. Russian sage, too, still offers graceful panicles of lavender-blue flowers.

As a background and filler of foliage, the blue-green of rue still looks fresh. Stalks of pale green soft-leaved apple mint could be used, and sweet cicely with its delicate and fragrant fernlike leaves. There is dark green tansy, and clusters of silvery green and purple-tinged sage leaves.

For a more boldly colored yellow and white bouquet, my friend could cut sprays of goldenrod (some are not yet tinged with brown) and the perennial sunflower, *Helianthus salicifolius*, which is in its prime up by the barn. The flowers of this tall, willowy daisy are a strong golden yellow, but the delicacy of their shape and gracefulness of habit relieve the harshness of their color. Against a white barn or in a vase with white flowers, they are marvelous. Annual sunflowers continue to bloom in the vegetable garden, the small-flowered creamy yellow ones called 'Italian White'. *Helenium* 'Butterpat' is here too, still offering secondary stalks of small fringed daisies.

These autumn yellows could be mixed nicely with white panicles of *Boltonia*, spires of burnet, and the russet leaves and white berries of our native gray dogwood.

For smaller bouquets, there are the last sweet blooms of the roses — 'Jacques Cartier' and 'Comte de Chambord', offering a few swirled pink flowers (and a final chance this season to smell that rich old rose fragrance), and 'Sea Foam', blooming indefatigably, its clusters of small white flowers now flushed with pink.

Hall's honeysuckle is flowering again on the herb garden arbor. The tubular cream and yellow blossoms, smelling of southern summers, could be used in boutonnieres or woven into nosegays for the bridal party.

❧

SOME
LITTLE
BULBS

It is not too late to plant some bulbs of lesser-known flowers for patches of delight in the garden next spring.

The striped squill, *Puschkinia scilloides*, is one I finally got

Puschkinia scilloides

around to planting last fall. E. A. Bowles describes it as "a pretty little gray thing like the ghost of a scilla come back to earth." It is not quite gray, more the palest white-blue (the color, Louise Beebe Wilder says, of skimmed milk), and the lovely racemes of six-petaled stars indeed have a transparent ghostlike delicacy compared with the bright blue scillas. The starry flowers face out, not downward, and are packed closely on their stems. Each petal, or segment, is marked by a sky-blue stripe inside and out, and these join together at the base of the flower to form a tube of the same soft blue. *Scilla tubergeniana* is similar in coloring, but its petals are more loosely arranged, and delicate separate filaments protrude from the center. The filaments of the *Puschkinia* are gathered together in a pale yellow cone. Growing about six inches high above grass-green basal leaves, *Puschkinia* is a bulb for an intimate spot in a sunny border. It is an appealing subject too for potting and forcing into bloom indoors in the winter.

The leucojums, or snowflakes, are like tall, stout snowdrops, and if they bloomed at the same time, I would not like them half as much. But on their own, blooming later in the spring, they have an undeniable charm. I have seen leucojums planted in wondrous quantity in the south of England, used as a ground cover the way we would plant lilies of the valley, and when in bloom in April under picturesque old magnolias and cherries, they were an envious sight. Here at Duck Hill, I content myself with a few tiny patches of snowflakes in shaded borders and in our wood.

Leucojum vernum, the spring snowflake, is first to bloom, soon after the snowdrops have faded. The bells are not teardrop-shaped like those of snowdrops, but are fatter, more like tiny upside-down bowls, their rounded petals ending in slight points that are tipped with green. Often two flowers hang from the six-inch stalks above glossy broad green leaves.

The summer snowflake, *L. aestivum*, blooms not in summer here, but in early May. It is a good deal taller in flower than *L. vernum*, with a series of bells down each stalk, and is lovely to see in small colonies where the soil is rich and damp. For several years after I planted my summer snowflakes, they did not bloom, and I was on the point of despairing, when suddenly one spring there they were, plump white bells dangling prettily on their stems in the shadow of an old apple tree near the woodland path. They are increasing slowly, enough to tempt me to cut a few for a slender pitcher indoors.

A May-flowering bulb, delightful for cutting as well as for ornamenting the garden, is our native *Camassia quamash* (sometimes in catalogs called *C. esculenta*). It has loose racemes of purple-blue stars on spikes that grow a foot or two tall. I would love to see it in its natural setting in the mountains of the Northwest, where it colors vast stretches of damp meadowland. On a more modest scale, the camassias grow without fuss in a rich garden bed in sun or light shade and can be inserted among clumps of perennials and May tulips to the enhancement of its neighbors.

Another bulb native to our West Coast that was new to me last fall is *Brodiaea laxa* (also called *Triteleia laxa*). It has the delicacy of an early spring flower but does not bloom until late May or early June. Soft purple tubular stars open from deeper purple buds and are borne in umbels a foot or more high above grassy leaves.

A small colony of *Brodiaea* (the variety 'Queen Fabiola') is planted in my herb garden, and until it blooms, I cannot tell its grassy leaves from those of the garlic chives through which it is woven. But the pale purple flowers bring early interest to this spot and perfectly echo the color of the catmint and lavender blooming at the same time nearby. It would be lovely to plant this native flower in a silver, blue, and white

Brodiaea laxa

garden, tucked in among front perennials of good foliage (like catmint) to mask its own insignificant leaves.

THE AGING PERENNIAL GARDEN

It is nine years since I planted the main garden, and it needs an overhaul. Whole sections need to be dug up (being careful not to disturb the shrub roses and peonies), turned over, enriched with compost and manure, and replanted.

I am astonished to realize how this garden has changed over the years. Some perennials that flourished in the early years (several kinds of yarrow, pinks, peachbells, and summer-blooming veronicas) have all but disappeared, and other plants have surreptitiously taken over. Tansy and the artemisias are advancing from the back of the borders. Apple mint crops up where it does not belong. Asters shove aside gentler plants in their wake. And the weeds! Certain grasses have gotten a foothold in the borders with roots going deep, thrusting their way up through clumps of iris and phlox. Ground ivy romps beneath roses and peonies and vies with lady's mantle and cranesbills along the front borders. Violets appear all over the place.

I heartily wish sometimes that I were an Edwardian lady with a staff of stalwart garden helpers at my side; I, in my long dress, would graciously instruct these workers and cheer them on as they dug up the plants, carefully laid them on burlap by the garden beds, then turned and dressed the soil, readying it for replanting. (Of course, I would not be content to stand there for long in my elegant dress — I would be down on my hands and knees gently pulling apart the plants that were to be returned to the beds, helping to plant them, before long grabbing a shovel to dig the hole just so, and tamping in the plant to my liking.)

Because there is no army of workers and because I do not have the physical energy I had fifteen or twenty years ago, the overhauling of the beds is done piecemeal, a patch at a time; and although the effect is not as dramatic, sooner or later the job is done.

How gratefully most perennials respond to new quarters! They revel in the new air and rich soil, and they thrive on being pulled apart and replanted in small pieces. There are a few exceptions, besides peonies, that prefer not to be disturbed. I leave baptisia and false dittany alone and rarely lift the snakeroots or Canadian burnet. Daylilies are left unsplit if I don't want to extend them, and usually so are the hostas. Old-fashioned bleeding heart and sweet cicely require no dividing and replanting. But most perennials grow and flower with renewed vigor and health after such a renovation.

In the process of overhauling a bed, bulbs are invariably dug up. If the job is done in September or early October, the bulbs can be quickly replanted with no harm done. In the spring this is more of a problem, because the bulbs are in an active state of growth and flowering and are best left undisturbed. So when I overhaul a patch in the spring, I go around the bulbs if I can.

The question is often asked whether to revamp a garden bed in the spring or fall. In our climate, each season has advantages and disadvantages. The soil is in ideal condition for digging in the autumn, but many of our less stalwart perennials, if lifted and divided now, fail to survive the winter. And in the spring we are at the mercy of our fickle weather. There are rarely more than a few brief and hectic weeks between the time that the beds thaw and dry out enough to be dug and our first heat wave with temperatures in the nineties.

I think the best advice is to do the job when you can, when the spirit moves you, when you have the spare time. This is true for so much of gardening. The rules about when to do something apply only if it is convenient. Do the job when you can rather than not at all.

❦

AUTUMN
COLORS

It seems to happen virtually overnight. Suddenly, in mid-October, the landscape is transformed into a magical patchwork of colors, a kaleidoscope of soft muted tones and brilliant flashes that make our Northeast autumns justly famous.

The glorious sugar maples set the stage, turning Halloween colors — pumpkin and gold. Swamp maples are flushed with crimson, ash and locust pale to soft yellow, and the great oak trees change slowly from deep green to a rich rust red.

The winged euonymus bushes that dress our roadsides are tinted rose pink, bush dogwoods turn russet and purple, and the barberries, as they shed their leaves, are a haze of red from

VIRGINIA CREEPER

ripened fruit. Even that gangling weed, sumac, is a splendid sight just now. On gravelly hillsides where the suckering shrub spreads unhampered, it paints vast pools of crimson color, equaled in intensity only by the swamp maple and the graceful Virginia creeper that clothes fence posts and tree trunks with its blaze of red.

Two dreaded weeds that romp over our stone walls and choke our trees are momentarily forgiven for the good color they add to the autumn spectacle: poison ivy in a bright golden garb sometimes tinged with red, and bittersweet, turned from green to pale butter yellow and peppered with clusters of gilded berries.

The woods are strangely sunlit by the leaves of maple and beech filtering through the branches and covering the woodland floor like golden confetti. On a gray, damp day they give an odd and lovely glow, an illusion of sunshine, as we walk along the paths there.

❧

WINDING
DOWN

My enthusiasm for weeding and tending the garden dwindles considerably by the middle of October. The garden beds are often cold and damp from frosty nights and heavy morning dews, the flowers are beginning to fade, leaves are falling heavily on the lawn; and, although there is much yet to do (raking and cutting down perennials, tidying edges, and planting bulbs), I am easily lured away from my responsibilities. A certain lethargy comes over me, a winding down perhaps, like fall itself, and when I should be tackling the myriad end-of-season tasks, I am tempted instead to take long sauntering walks, savoring the beauty of the bigger landscape.

This year, however, I have a special excuse for shirking my garden duties. We have a new puppy, a three-month-old Scottish deerhound named Maisie, and all effort in the garden has become complicated in her presence. She is quite unruly still, a lop-eared, pouncing, playful goof of a dog, and, although she is sweet-natured and often eager to please, her

attention span is short and she moves quickly from one exasperating prank to the next. My gardening gloves and tools disappear as I bend over to pull some weeds, my essential kneepad is whisked away as I get up to empty a basket, and the leaves and stalks carefully placed in that basket are pulled out and strewn about the lawn.

Maisie considers the garden beds, with their light rich soil, perfect for digging, and if she sees me with a spade or trowel, she is delighted to find I like digging, too. I sneak off to tuck some bulbs in a bed while she is busy with a stick, but within seconds she has discovered me and wants to help, working the loosened soil feverishly with her front paws, quickly dislodging the bulbs I have just planted. In exasperation, I tie her to the wheelbarrow, which she promptly tips over, then stands there looking pitiful until I relent and let her go. Great muddy paws embrace me in thanks.

It is a farce, a slapstick comedy, and I long for the gardening chores to be over. By next spring, if I am lucky, she will be grown-up, calm, perfectly behaved, happy to lie picturesquely by my side (front paws elegantly crossed) as I go about my garden tasks.

ᚱᚷ

RED-LEAVED
PLANTS

On the whole, I am not crazy about red- and purple-leaved plants — that is, plants with red or purple foliage throughout the growing seasons. I object to them especially in the spring; they seem wrong then with all the fresh green, almost as though they were there by mistake, were meant for the autumn season instead. In summer their deep tones of copper, maroon, and plum are more pleasing to the eye, creating depth and shadow in the bolder, brighter garden. By fall they are barely noticeable, lesser participants in the panorama of colors, similar to many other dusky hues of the season, a somber background for the flashes of scarlet and orange and yellow.

Why do Americans plant so many dark red and purple-leaved shade trees? To me they have a heavy, lugubrious look to them. I think in particular of the reddish purple and dark purple-brown varieties of the Norway maple that are so extensively planted today. How much pleasanter, more fresh and natural are their green-leaved counterparts!

I feel the same way about beech trees; our native beech (*Fagus grandifolia*) is such a glorious tree, and the green-leaved European beech is preferable in most cases, I think, to its purple form. Admittedly, the copper beech in its maturity, standing alone in a vast park or estate, is an impressive sight. From my childhood near Philadelphia, I associate copper beeches with gloomy Victorian mansions, for they were a common accompaniment, and often intensified the daunting atmosphere of these places.

Some of the purple-leaved plums and crabapples have a sharpness to their coloring that does not seem in harmony with the gentleness of spring. This is particularly true when they are seen in company with ornamental trees and shrubs that have ordinary green foliage. Russell Page, in his book *The Education of a Gardener*, suggests that the purple-leaved fruit trees are most successful when grouped with "other plants in the same dusky range of color."

Similarly, red- and purple-leaved shrubs can be effective in the garden when grouped together rather than planted as single specimens in a border of green. Right now I am removing a red-leaved Japanese barberry (*Berberis thunbergii atropurpurea*) from the nasturtium border where it has been jarring my eye all spring and summer. It looked like a blob of dark color plunked down in the middle of the border for no reason, relating to nothing, surrounded as it was on all sides by green-leaved shrubs and perennials. This particular barberry has a cold purplish cast to its red leaves — a deep maroon with a film of blue in most lights — and, although the foliage complements red flowers (crimson and scarlet) splendidly, it looked harsh to my eye with all the gold flowers that predominate in this small border. (Curiously, the May flowers of the red-leaved barberry are that same strong yellow and seem to fight with the color of its leaves.)

Another time I would plant a grouping of red-leaved Japanese barberries together with the plum-colored *Rosa glauca* in the back of a red border, or with pink and chartreuse flowers, the colors of cranesbills and lady's mantle. (A gardening friend of mine has a stunning border where she has mixed masses of the red-leaved barberry, mostly in its dwarf form, with flowers of cool pink and magenta, lavender blue, and yellow-green.)

I admit to a special fondness for the purple smokebush (*Cotinus coggygria* 'Royal Purple'). The leaves are not really purple at all but a rich reddish brown, with shadings of plum and green, that complements red flowers handsomely. Growing in a bed beside the vegetable garden arbor, my bush serves as a backdrop for a succession of fiery flowers. Red tulips in spring are followed by a drift of old-fashioned double Oriental poppies, colored a vivid orange-red. Later the bright orange lily 'Connecticut Yankee' and an assortment of scarlet annuals continue the color scheme. If you can site this shrub where the afternoon sun filters through its leaves, giving them an almost translucent quality, then you will see the smokebush at its most beautiful.

It is a big shrub, growing to ten feet or more in my garden, even though I cut it back ruthlessly every spring. The large, fluttery leaves are held loosely on their stems, and the branches themselves billow out gracefully, saving it from the heavy look of many red- and purple-leaved shrubs and trees. In autumn the smokebush forsakes its more somber tones and turns bright with patches of copper and scarlet.

PURPLE SMOKEBUSH
(*Cotinus coggygria*)

Plants with green leaves that are merely tinged with dark red or purple I find infinitely easier to place effectively in the garden. The emerging leaves of many trees in spring are attractively burnished with red (the black cherry and our crabapples come quickly to mind). Peonies have this advantage as they unfold in May and are a wonderful contrast to the burgeoning greens and grays around them. Astilbes have russet foliage, too, before they unfurl in early spring.

The red-leaved barberry when grown in shade is much greener in leaf (here it is merely flushed with red), and I find its lighter look more pleasing. The lovely *Rosa glauca* is another good example of green foliage brushed with plum and gray and copper to good effect.

In summer the ruby-colored lettuces are festive foliage plants to combine with the brilliant flowers of nasturtiums and French marigolds or with the infinite variations of green in other vegetables. Purple sage, its pale green pebbly leaves streaked with soft purple, is another striking and useful foliage plant in the garden. It flatters almost any other color, from gold to chartreuse, scarlet to candy pink, magenta to lavender blue.

❧

THE COMPOST HEAP

I have a friend who lives in the middle of the city and has a wonderful garden there, a magical retreat from the noise and asphalt and hurly-burly just outside her front door. It is quite small by country standards, no more than fifty feet long and twenty feet wide, a mixture of small trees and shrubs, perennials and bulbs, interlaced with paths.

Even in this confined area, where every inch of space is valuable, my friend has a compost heap. It is contained in a bin and hidden behind a shrub in a corner of the garden, and here she collects her leaves and clippings and occasional donations of manure from our barnyard.

I laughed, on a visit one fall, to see her delicately pick up a single leaf that had fallen on her path and carry it, like some sliver of gold, to her compost bin. Laughed knowing that at home leaves were falling like confetti, that there would be mountains of leaves, a seemingly endless supply, to rake into piles and drag away to our compost area. But the results are the same, and in a year's time, my city friend and I will have lovely loose soillike humus to put back in our gardens.

I think the compost heap does not have to be an elaborate production. Even without the advised turning and wetting down, a pile of leaves and weeds and grass clippings will decompose within a year's time (the blessed earthworms help

the process along) and be usable as a mulch in the garden. I keep three piles going behind some trees and shrubs near the white garden. One pile is for dumping on this year, a second pile is last year's accumulation in the process of decomposing, and a third pile is two years old and being shoveled back into the garden.

If you have a spot behind a shrub, not too far from the garden, where you can start a heap, by all means do. It is astonishing how quickly that mountain of leaves settles down and begins to disintegrate. And the end result is a splendid tonic for the garden beds. In a time when we are becoming increasingly conscious of the problems of our mounting waste and are turning to recycling as a solution, it is satisfying to think of all those weeds and discarded clippings and leaves from the garden easily transformed into a treasure of crumbly dark brown compost.

November

BITTERSWEET

Heavy rain and wind have caused most of the trees to shed their leaves. The distant hills are washed now with pastel tones — soft purples and grays, interrupted only by the deep green of an occasional pine grove and the rust-brown of the oak. There is a sudden starkness to the countryside, a baring of bones, and any lingering color of leaf or flower or berry is especially savored.

Almost alone among our native deciduous trees, the great oaks hold onto their coppery foliage sometimes well into winter. The weeping willows, too, are slow to drop their leaves; they become marvelous brush strokes of golden yellow in the dulling November landscape.

Bittersweet, that decorative, festive symbol of autumn, is in its prime, leafless now, its winding branches heavy with clusters of gold capsules flared open to reveal fleshy vermilion fruit. The pale gray branches of winterberry are still littered with glossy red berries, and great mounded bushes of the multiflora rose are a tangle of glowing red hips.

Our native witch hazel, *Hamamelis virginiana*, which

237

abounds in the understory of neighboring woods, is in full flower, studded all over with little yellow tassels. It is a startling sight, on a November walk, to suddenly come upon these graceful shrubs, flowering now in the lateness of fall.

At Duck Hill there are still some satisfying patches of color. The purple smokebush is in its final glory, splashed with pink and orange and crimson, at its best when the late afternoon sun shines through the leaves. Three bushes of dwarf fothergilla (*F. gardenii*), planted in our new courtyard, are mottled handsomely with red and orange. Privet is still an astonishing fresh green and peppered with smoky blue-black berries. Forsythia is shaded with purple, the rugosa roses are a soft yellow, and viburnums and dogwoods are flushed with russet and red.

Some tall, unfashionable daisy-type chrysanthemums are blooming cheerfully in the garden. Unfashionable because, as far as I know, these late-flowering willowy varieties are no longer available from nurseries. Perhaps the nurserymen think that no one will buy flowers that do not bloom in the garden until late October and November. I saw them first on a chilly November day some years ago in a friend's garden and admired them (in fact, lusted for them), astonished to find fresh blooms so late in the gardening season. With typical gardeners' generosity, pots of freshly dug divisions arrived on my doorstep the following spring. Now these charming lavender-pink and butter-yellow daisies are the mainstay of my early November bouquets and the last real splash of flower color in my garden beds.

In a mild November the white and yellow fumitories continue to flower in the gravel and cracks of the stone steps, and catmint throws out fresh shoots of lavender blooms. Johnny-jump-ups can be found scattered about the garden, and in sheltered sunny nooks the mauve-pink violet reblooms.

Some of the woody plants in the herb garden, like germander, lavender, santolina, and thyme, retain their foliage colors through fall and early winter, and their patterns of gray and green, framed now by the reddened barberry hedge, make a pleasingly colorful late autumn picture.

ON
ROSE
GARDENS

While planting a rose bush in the main garden (early November and the beginning of April are the best times in our climate to plant shrub roses that arrive bare-rooted in the mail), I have been thinking about gardens devoted to roses and how they are most successfully arranged.

A visit to a small public rose garden nearby this past June brought home to me how unprepossessing a garden of roses can look if it is not softened by other plants. This garden had an interesting collection of old shrub roses, floribundas, and hybrid teas (with climbers and ramblers on metal arches) that were a pleasure to see for their individual beauty. But they were planted starkly in bare earth in a pattern of narrow beds plunked down in a field of grass. No edging, no underplanting, no hedges were used to enhance the roses. And I thought at the time, how sad not to have taken the trouble to frame those beautiful rose blooms with an edging of boxwood or some fragrant herb and enclose the whole garden with a fence or hedge of yew or hemlock.

Roses by nature are leggy shrubs, often gaunt and awkward in shape, and they need a frame of some other good-looking foliage to set them off and make a pleasing picture. Hybrid teas are the worst offenders, stiff and upright, their fabulous blooms held without grace. But even the old shrub roses, though they often weep attractively, have a basically leggy disposition. And the blooms of roses all by themselves, as Graham Stuart Thomas has pointed out, can (from any distance) have a spotty effect.

All of this can be simply solved by providing the garden with a suitable background and surrounding the rose beds with a low hedge. Boxwood would be my first choice to border the roses. It is a traditional edging in a rose garden, and the dense, rich green foliage, clipped to a neat geometric line or allowed its natural mounded shape, is a handsome frame for the vibrant rose blooms.

But there are less expensive alternatives. Germander makes a superb low hedge similar to boxwood when clipped, although the small glossy leaves are not evergreen in our climate. Hyssop is another herb that is eminently suited to hedging and would make an attractive edging for roses. It is hardier than germander and leafs out earlier in the spring, with upright branches of bright green lanceolate leaves that clip easily into a prim rectangular hedge.

Lavender is an appropriate companion for roses, and a hedge of the billowing gray leaves and purple spikes is always pleasing in a rose garden. For a more informal, less structured edging, cottage pinks (*Dianthus plumarius*) and catmint (*Nepeta* × *faassenii*) make a charming border. I think if I were using gray-leaved plants to border the roses, I would be sure to surround the garden with a hedge of dark green — yew would be ideal, or Japanese holly or, if there was room, Canadian hemlock.

A rose garden can, of course, include a mixture of other plants among the roses. A splendid example of this is the rose garden at Mottisfont Abbey in Hampshire, England, where Graham Stuart Thomas has gathered the National Trust's collection of historic roses. They are artistically planted in large beds, mostly edged with box, where the roses mingle with foxgloves, campanulas, and alliums and are underplanted with lady's mantle, pinks, and violas. At Sissinghurst, too, the rose garden is in truth a mixture of perennials and shrubs and bulbs carpeting the ground and weaving through a profusion of roses.

The older varieties of roses (damask, alba, gallica, centifolia, bourbon, and hybrid perpetual) are particularly suited to this mixed planting because of their more graceful shapes and masses of flowers. But many of our more modern roses can be successfully interwoven with other shrubs and perennials and bulbs. The rugosas are an obvious choice, with their dense shape, handsome foliage, and long season of flower and fruit.

The hybrid musks are another group of roses nicely suited to mixed planting. In habit they are somewhere between a lax climber and a shrub, with loose, gracefully arching canes and clusters of flowers in lovely fragile tones that continue to open through fall. (Alas, they are marginally hardy for me here, and rarely survive a severe winter.) And now it seems that the rose hybridists are interested in creating a new line of hardy roses that are not only long-blooming but have a graceful shrublike habit and masses of flowers. Yearly we are introduced to new rose selections that could be effectively combined in a garden with other flowers.

This mixed planting is certainly one way of creating a pleasing picture with roses. But if you want a garden of just roses — a rose garden pure and simple — then I urge you to consider your background (create a wall or hedge or fence), choose a pattern of beds that pleases your eye, plant your roses closely so they will interweave, and then bind these beds with a beautiful small hedge, a ribbon of greenery.

❧

ARBORS

In today's typical small garden, where there is often more desire for flowers than room to contain them, one solution is to think vertically. Walls, fences, posts, tree trunks, shed roofs, and porch railings can be hosts to a variety of flowering vines that have been coaxed to climb them. Here is a chance to grow climbing and rambling roses, clematis, honeysuckle, wisteria, and hydrangea — a great show of flowers — using a minimum of ground space.

One of the most delightful structures for adding this flowery dimension to the garden is the arbor. Fortunately, it is not at all difficult to find a spot where one would be suitable. An arbor can mark a passageway from one garden area to another, shade a bench or seat at the end of a path, or stand

above a gate where the garden is entered. If a rustic arbor will do, it can be built, without the expertise of a carpenter, from wood gathered from your property if you have it, or some begged from a friend. And when covered with masses of roses or dripping with wisteria, this charming structure will add not only color and scent but a touch of romance to the garden.

There are two rustic arbors at Duck Hill, one casting shade on a bench in the herb garden, the second framing the gate at the entrance to the vegetable garden. They were built by my sons and me from wood cut down when we were clearing our small paddock. Many of the young trees were black locusts, which are ideal for arbor-making. (Any hard wood will do, the harder the better.) The trunks furnished the uprights and crosspieces of the arbor, then smaller branches were used to make a pattern on the arbor's sides. (For inspiration we turned to photographs of Edwardian gardens, where so many structures were fashioned from rustic wood.)

It is best to make the arbor higher than you think it needs to be (seven feet is a minimum), for when it is dripping with flowers and foliage it will seem a good deal smaller, and you don't want to feel you have to duck when you walk underneath it.

Arbors are ideal structures for rambling roses. They love the air and sun that these free-standing supports afford, and their long pliant canes are easily wound around the posts and will tumble gracefully from the uppermost timbers. In the Northeast, where most of our houses are built of painted wood, making them impractical surfaces for covering with roses, arbors are the perfect alternative for growing the enchanting ramblers.

Clematis can be woven in among the ramblers' many canes to extend their flowery show. Or the more vigorous varieties of clematis can clothe the arbor alone. Our vegetable garden arbor is a cloud of white in September when the sweet autumn clematis (*C. paniculata*) is in bloom, covering it with masses of tiny starry flowers.

Several beautiful varieties of honeysuckle would willingly weave up and over an arbor, but none that I know of smells better than the common Hall's honeysuckle, which winds up the side of the arbor in our herb garden. This Japanese honeysuckle has become a formidable woodland weed in this area and south of here; like bittersweet and escaped seedlings of wisteria, it can kill trees with its ever-tightening stranglehold. But when it is confined to the stout limbs of the arbor, I forget its menace and enjoy the wafts of sweet fragrance from its soft yellow and white flowers in June and again in a mild fall.

❦

VARIEGATED
FOLIAGE

I am surprised to discover sometimes that gardeners whose judgment I respect despise variegated plants. Fussy, unnatural, diseased-looking, they call them. And yet to me, variegated foliage is invariably appealing. I admit that a garden made up solely of striped and splotched leaves would be busy and distracting. But when planted with discretion — that is, surrounded by a greater quantity of solid green leaves — variegated plants are often delightfully decorative. Their value in the garden is similar to that of gray plants; they tend to lighten up a planting, especially in half-shaded places, and at times seem almost flowerlike in their effect.

When we speak of variegated foliage, we are usually referring to green or blue-green leaves edged or otherwise marked (in stripes or splotches) with a paler color — the palest green or gray, pale yellow, cream, or white. It is this lightening of the foliage that gives it such interest, particularly when juxtaposed with solid green leaves.

There are a number of perennials and shrubs at Duck Hill that I value for their lively variegated leaves. Among deciduous shrubs, *Daphne* × *burkwoodii* 'Carol Mackie' is at the top of my list of favorites, with whorls of narrow dark green leaves that are boldly edged in pale yellow. This small shrub holds on to its leaves well into winter and is a splendid companion here for plump bushes of boxwood.

Cornus alba 'Elegantissima' is an attractive and useful red-twigged dogwood with variegated leaves of soft green edged in creamy white. The plain-leaved red-stemmed dogwoods are probably best grown in masses in the wilder parts of the garden, where their bright red branches can be appreciated in winter. But this dressier variety is well suited to the more

Daphne × *burkwoodii* 'CAROL MACKIE'

formal garden. It is easily contained to a bush four or five feet high and wide, and it has a graceful habit, making it a good subject for the back of the flower border. Here, in a corner of the white garden, it makes an elegant backdrop for a succession of blue and white flowers. It would look equally well with yellow flowers (I would like a border one day of just yellow, green, and white) or mingled with scarlet flowers in a red and white border, its own crimson branches carrying the theme into winter.

Kerria japonica 'Picta' is another variegated shrub that can be nicely incorporated into the flower border. It is rather small in size and has the typical delicate saw-toothed kerria leaf, in this case prettily edged with white. The single golden roselike flowers open in May and look particularly light-hearted against the green and white foliage. It is a good idea, however, to keep in mind the strong yellow of these flowers when placing this kerria in the garden. Although its ornamental leaves complement any flower color, when the bush is in bloom, it is best kept away from candy-pink flowers. Place it with soft purply blues and white, or in a bold golden yellow border, or mixed with other fiery sunset hues.

I have craved a bush of variegated boxwood ever since I saw a sprig of it one evening in the buttonhole of an eminent and very dapper gardening gentleman. There are two sorts to be had: *Buxus sempervirens* 'Argenteo-variegata' with leaves edged in silvery white; and 'Aureo-variegata', its small dark green leaves edged with pale yellow. I now have a small bush of the latter (received through the mail), which struggles to survive the vagaries of our winters. It is growing at a snail's pace in a sheltered spot in the vegetable garden (a violent plunge in temperature early last winter killed back several years of top growth), and I despair sometimes that it will ever be big enough to take its place in the garden scheme. How I envy my dapper evening companion, who boasted of a big bush of this boxwood in his much-warmer-zoned garden on Long Island.

A few perennials with variegated leaves mixed in with solid green and gray-green plants bring a sparkle to most garden schemes. Lungwort (*Pulmonaria saccharata*) brightens damp half-shaded beds even when it is not in bloom because of its polka-dotted leaves — the palest green splotches and dots on a background of dark green. Countless varieties of variegated hosta are dramatically effective in the garden. I like to use them as a front edging in shaded beds or massed as a ground cover in less formal areas.

In the herb garden, several different thymes and mints create light and pattern with their variegation. Silver thyme is a low-growing, clump-forming kind with small pale green leaves edged in white, which indeed gives a silvery effect to a border where it is used. Golden lemon thyme is similar in habit, but its lemon-scented green leaves are tipped with yellow. 'Doone's Valley' is a prostrate thyme to grow in the crevices of rocks; the tiny dark green leaves are splotched with golden yellow in spring. As summer advances, the variegation fades away.

I grow pineapple mint for its patterned leaves — soft gray-green marked boldly with white. Ginger mint (cherished for its delicious scent) has smooth, dark green leaves nicely streaked with yellow. I have discovered that it is best to dig up, divide, and replant these mints often to keep their leaves from losing their colorful markings.

Golden sage, a low-growing, variegated cultivar of the

common cooking sage, has pale green leaves strikingly marked with yellow. Several clumps of this sage planted together have a beautiful effect combined with the contrasting foliage of other herbs and the mauve and lavender-purple flowers that abound in this garden.

There are all sorts of scented geraniums whose leaves are edged and splotched with white or pale yellow. They have the same decorative value as flowers, and endless combinations can be thought up to use them attractively in the garden beds or in pots and window boxes.

I have a list of variegated plants seen in other people's gardens that I long to have at Duck Hill. I want the tall handsome grass *Miscanthus sinensis* 'Variegatus' to plant up by the barn with golden sunflowers. I am mulling over where I could put the lovely *Iris pallida* that is slashed with pale yellow or white. Variegated Solomon's seal would be nice to lighten a patch of our woodland. I have been meaning to designate a spot (protected from the deer) for the trailing euonymus *E. fortunei* 'Silver Queen', which is edged in white, not only to brighten a bit of gloomy ground, but to cut for autumn and winter bouquets.

I doubt if it ever ends, this desire for new plants. It is part of the fun and excitement of gardening.

A
REMARKABLE
RABBIT

We have a remarkable rabbit named Andy. Although he is unmistakably a pet, with his black and white markings, he is free now to go where he wants; his days are spent by the garden or in the barnyard, but at night he disappears to some secret shelter in the wild.

This has not always been the case. For at least a year, Andy lived in a sybaritic pen (by pet-rabbit standards) that we built for raising chickens. An indoor house soft with shavings and lit by small windows led to an outdoor pen perfect for hopping around or lying stretched out in the sun.

But Andy became restless and started to spend hours digging tunnels with his nose and paws. Eventually the tunnels led under the wire fence to freedom. At first we would catch him each time he escaped (this took several people and a well-thought-out strategy, for he is amazingly quick and clever). In the end we realized that we either had to lock him up in the small rabbit hutch inside the barn or let him have his freedom. We chose the latter course, knowing his long-term chances of survival were slim but feeling that at least he would be briefly, gloriously happy.

That was several months ago. Miraculously, Andy lives on, spending his days with the chickens and ducks and barn cats, then, soon after dusk, disappearing into the shadows. Neighbors say they have seen him going in and out of a woodchuck hole down the road. By morning he is back, hopping up the driveway as we go to feed the horses.

Our large old hunter (he is part Clydesdale, with the shaggy pasterns and huge hooves typical of the draft horse) lives outside in the small paddock by the barn, and has the chickens and ducks and Andy as company when he gets his feed. He is a gentle soul and does not seem to mind that they stand by his feet and eat the bits of grain he drops. It looks like a romanticized Victorian painting of a barnyard scene.

❧

PAPER-WHITES
AND
HYACINTHS

I wonder, are my husband and I the only ones who find the smell of paper-white narcissus unbearably cloying in the confines of a small room? All the rooms at Duck Hill are small and cozy, and as a consequence, for a number of years I gave up growing these charming, easy bulbs for winter flowering.

But now I am happily potting them up again to flower on our new sun porch. This is not a room where we spend much time sitting — it serves really as our entrance hall — and because the room is cool and breezy (from the front door being continually opened and closed), the scent of the paper-whites will not be overpowering. All in all a welcome solution, for I love the delicate look of these tender daffodils and have missed having pots of them standing about to dress the house in December and January.

They are the easiest bulbs in the world to force into bloom, not even requiring the usual few weeks of dark and cool temperatures. Plunked down halfway in a pot or bowl of soil or pebbles, they will immediately put forth their fresh green straplike leaves and, in a few weeks' time with good light, will magically produce their small, elegant clusters of starry white flowers.

The Chinese sacred lily is not a lily at all, but another tender narcissus as easy to force as paper-whites. It has tight clusters of small, rounded yellow and white flowers and a fragrance similar to the paper-white's but not quite as strong.

I like to put a few clay pots of delicate narcissus with a lighter, more enjoyable fragrance in the cold frame in October, to bring into our snug rooms in flower during February and March. 'Liberty Bells' is a charming sort that is readily available, with dainty nodding flowers (usually two to a stem) of lemon yellow and a light tangy scent. The miniature triandrus 'Hawera' has clusters of tiny pendent pale yellow flowers with flared-back petals that rise above tall grasslike leaves and have a strong but appealing perfume.

CHINESE SACRED LILY

Hyacinths are almost as easy as paper-whites to force into flower, and what a breath of spring color and fragrance they bring to a windowsill in January or February! I find the graceful multiflora varieties of hyacinths particularly suited to pot culture. They lack the stiffness of the big Dutch hybrids; the flowers are smaller and more loosely held, and several flowering spikes rise and sway above their broad ribbed foliage. These hyacinths are available in white, lavender blue, or candy pink — all of them lighthearted and alluring, with a strong but not overpowering honeylike fragrance. The bulbs are quite large — three fit nicely in a six- or seven-inch bulb pot — and require only a moderate period (about eight weeks) of dark and cool temperatures before they are ready to coax into bloom.

The cost of florists' flowers to fill one vase in winter is staggering, and their beauty fleeting. How much more desirable (and clever to boot) to have instead, for a fraction of the cost and a little effort, pots of long-blooming spring flowers that will bring color and charm and fragrance to our winter rooms.

December

INKBERRY
(Ilex glabra)

Sometime in the beginning of December, with the approach of the holidays a constant refrain, I look around Duck Hill and wish I had more evergreens. How nice it is to have your own greens to fashion into wreaths and garlands for decorating the doors and mantels and tables at Christmas time. I make urgent notes in my garden diary to plant more inkberry and pieris and holly, and to (please!) find a spot for some feathery junipers.

Often we Northeasterners tend to err on the side of too many evergreens in our yards — great spruces towering above the rooftops, yews crowded by the windows, rhododendrons huddled along the driveway, miserably curled in our frigid weather. When we first came to Duck Hill, we were faced with a few typical ill-placed, overgrown specimens. An immense and ratty Norway spruce loomed drearily over the south end of the garden and was soon felled to bring in more light and air. I replaced a stiff block of yews planted against the east side of the house with lilacs and viburnums. An out-of-scale blue spruce was removed to make way for the

257

vegetable garden. This left us with two tattered rhododendrons (still on the demolition list), a plump clipped yew on
either side of the front door (which we cosset and carefully
protect from the deer), and an old Scotch pine that leans over
one corner of the herb garden. In essence, a dearth of evergreens. We have since planted hemlocks and box and holly to
enhance the gardens. But I lust for graceful groupings of
winter greenery along the perimeters of our property that
would afford me a variety of cuttings for holiday decorations.

Even after the holidays are over, the craving for evergreens
persists. In the long winter months, when the bare-boned
landscape is painted in shades of brown and gray, my eye
searches for patches of green and delights in their discovery.

In our local woods, clumps of dark green Christmas ferns
are good to see among the rocks and leaves. Sometimes we
come across a carpeting of the delicate princess pine, with its
curious bristly leaves and creamy beige candles. Only the
emerald moss that hugs the sides of rocks and tree stumps is a
brighter color.

The narrow Eastern red cedars (*Juniperus virginiana*) appear like solitary sentinels in our rolling fields, a somber olive
green often studded with smoky blue berries. Groves of white
pine stand majestically by the water's edge. This is one of the
most graceful of our big native evergreens, its straight tall
trunks prized in an earlier century for fashioning into ships'
masts. The lively green clusters of long needles are held on
dramatically sweeping branches, and the overall effect is one
of rich elegance. Another evergreen tree of lighthearted grace
is our Canadian hemlock, at its best when seen along the
rocky banks of a woodland stream, its feathery branches
swooping down as if to touch the running water. How prefer-

able these two great natives are to that overplanted and most mournful of evergreen trees, the Norway spruce, which in its maturity seems too tired to hold erect its long languid fingers of dark green.

Inkberry (*Ilex glabra*) is a native treasure, a loose billowing bush of lustrous green leaves that grows naturally in open swampy places. In the garden it will grow well in normal soil that is not too sunbaked and is an attractive alternative among broad-leaved evergreens, especially in its compact form, for planting near the house or massing at the edge of the garden with mountain laurel and andromeda.

The most elegant of our native evergreen shrubs, mountain laurel (*Kalmia latifolia*) spreads through the understory where oak trees abound, coloring the winter woodland with its rich green leathery leaves. In June it is spangled with beautiful clusters of bowl-shaped pink-and-white flowers. Mountain andromeda (*Pieris floribunda*) is a similar evergreen in leaf with attractive upright panicles of cream-white flowers that open in early spring from pink-tinged winter buds. It is a native of our southern states but is perfectly hardy for us here, a delightful small shrub to plant in shady parts of the garden. I prefer this American pieris to the more commonly seen Japanese andromeda, which has clusters of drooping flowers; but this, too, is an invaluable winter shrub to mass with other broad-leaved evergreens in light shade.

It is not until December that I truly appreciate pachysandra. This evergreen ground cover is so overplanted in our Northeast gardens that it is looked on with disdain, and we forget what a truly remarkable plant it is. All winter long the clusters of leaves are an extraordinary glossy rich green — I can think of no other ground cover that equals its color —

and pachysandra consents to grow, in fact thrives, in the dense shade and starved ground of our many maple trees. It is disease-free, never requires the least care, and continues year after year to put on a splendid show of green.

Periwinkle, *Vinca minor*, is a more highly regarded evergreen ground cover and, indeed, up close it is a prettier plant, with its graceful wandering stems of glossy leaves and lovely pinwheel flowers of lavender blue or white. But from a distance, its green has a cold look to it — the leaves have a silvery blue sheen that makes periwinkle not quite as satisfying an evergreen in the chill of winter.

In the country we don't use ivy as much as we might to cover the ground in formal places under shrubs. Several varieties of English ivy are hardy enough here, and although their green in winter is somber, they make a handsome carpet for deciduous shrubs in simple beds by the house.

It is an unfortunate fact that the majority of our evergreens are relished by the deer. You can always tell a deer-ridden area by the state of its evergreens. Yew and holly, hemlock and pine, rhododendron and mountain laurel will be stripped of leaves up to the height the deer can reach unless they have been carefully caged in with wire for the winter. This has not always been so. With an increase in the deer population and a decrease in their natural woodland habitat, these lovely creatures are learning more and more to rely on our garden plantings for their winter diet. There is no easy answer to our dilemma (hunting with guns or reintroducing natural predators have their obvious drawbacks); if we crave evergreens, we must either be content to plant the ones the deer don't eat (boxwood, Japanese andromeda, the Pfitzer juniper, spruce, and fir trees seem so far to be spurned) or take the trouble to protect our winter greenery with fences of wire.

‰

HERBS
ON THE
SUN
PORCH

All sorts of fragrant decorative herbs besides rosemary and geraniums flourish during winter on the sun porch. Three tender kinds of lavender are an elegant addition and often flower through the winter months. French lavender, or fringed lavender, (*Lavandula dentata*) has narrow, delicately toothed gray leaves (there is also a green-leaved variety) and lavender-purple flowers on short spikes. Spanish lavender, *L. stoechas* (also confusingly called French lavender) has short gray linear leaves and curious mauve-purple flowers with lavender bracts that are fatter than the usual lavender spikes and very showy. *L. multifida*, which blooms untiringly from October to March, doesn't look (or smell) much like a lav-

Lavandula multifida

ender at all. It does have long tapering spikes of bright purple flowers — sometimes several spikes to a stem — but its foliage is feathery and fernlike. The soft light green leaves have a sharp piny smell that is not unpleasant but does not hint of lavender the way we know it.

Santolina, or lavender cotton, is another pungent herb that seems to thrive on the sun porch. Its gray corallike leaves and dense mounded habit are decorative whether it is grown naturally in a pot or trained as a standard. It is easy to form into a small topiary tree and, because of its pale color, is a wonderful contrast to the dark green rosemaries.

Another herb that I have discovered makes nice topiary standards is germander. This is a quick-growing plant indoors, seemingly unbothered by bugs or disease, and the small shiny toothed leaves are easily clipped into a ball. Myrtle (*Myrtus communis*) has a similar look when trained to a standard but is much slower-growing. The large-leaved variegated myrtle is pleasant to grow naturally for its brightly patterned leaves and graceful habit.

Lemon verbena can be brought indoors; in fact, this is the only way to eventually have a big plant of it, for in our climate it is tender and will be lost if left outdoors. The sheer green leaves, when rubbed, release a sweet lemon scent that has no equal. Often lemon verbena loses its leaves in the fall and goes dormant for a few months. I leave it on the porch, keeping it slightly moist, for the bare twiggy branches are not unattractive. In February new light green leaves will emerge, and by spring it will be fully leaved again. Lemon verbena tends to get buggy indoors and needs a weekly swishing in soapy water to keep it healthy.

I like to have a pot of the slow-growing bay, *Laurus nobilis*, on the porch. Its dark leathery leaves are a pleasant contrast to all the lacier foliage around, and it is nice, too, for the chef to clip for his stews and soups.

Sometimes I dig up some tiny patches of creeping thyme to pot up for the winter. Woolly thyme spilling over a small clay pot is a delicious surprise for the eye and the nose on a snowy day.

FORMAL
GARDENS

Perhaps it is a sign of age. The older I get, the more I find I delight in the simplicity of formal gardens. There is a restfulness, a satisfaction to my eye in simple rows of trees and repeated geometric patterns — patterns etched out with trees and shrubs, clipped evergreens and hedges. Flowers are incidental to this kind of garden, merely added decoration, the icing on the cake. The beauty is in the garden's bones and is constant all year round.

One of the advantages of the formal garden, as Roy Strong points out in his excellent book on the subject, is that once it is established, it is fairly easy to maintain. Easier, that is, than a garden that relies solely on flowers for its show. Of course, this is not true of a formal garden on a grand scale — we are not talking about Versailles — but, rather, one that is small and intimate, more like the gardens of Elizabethan times or those in medieval cloisters or our own prim Colonial gardens. The initial effort and thought to create a formal garden are considerable, and the cost of the trees and evergreens and hedges that might make up your design could certainly be more than you would spend on a garden of flowers. But once the pattern is established, the stage set, less maintenance is needed to keep this garden presentable, and best of all, it can be counted on in all seasons to please the eye.

A formal garden can, indeed, be beautiful with no flowers at all, just greenery in geometric patterns with a tracery of trees and perhaps a statue or a distant view. But it can also serve as a framework for an exuberance of flowers. This is my vision for Duck Hill, where a love of formal lines must marry with a passion for gathering and growing flowers. Sissinghurst is possibly the most famous modern example of this type of garden. When it was created in the thirties, it was Harold Nicolson who insisted on the formal bones. He plotted the axes and created rooms and vistas with hedges and walls and lines of trees; then, within those strictures, Vita Sackville-West planted her romantic profusion of flowers.

At the beginning of the century, Gertrude Jekyll and Edwin Lutyens had a similar partnership. Lutyens built the gardens as extensions of his houses — handsome stone-walled terraces with bold formal arrangements of paths and stone steps, rills and pergolas. Gertrude Jekyll then proceeded to soften those strict formal lines with masses of billowing shrubs and herbs and flowers.

Our Colonial gardens were simpler in their design, quiet

and tidy, harking back more to Tudor gardens, with their homely collection of fruit trees and flowers and herbs confined in a pattern of small beds, often edged in boxwood. There was a charm in their unpretentious formality that seems appealing and appropriate today in our scaled-down, simplified gardens.

I think we should not be put off by thinking the formal garden too grand a concept for our times. It can be as modest, as simple, as you wish. Neat, long rows of vegetables framed by a low clipped hedge or arranged in a pattern of circles and squares can be as pleasing to the eye as the most intricate French parterre. And the grandest English avenue is no more satisfying than your own driveway lined on either side with sugar maples or flowering fruit trees.

TWO EVERGREEN BARBERRIES

I have two varieties of evergreen barberry that attractively dress a garden border at this time of year. Densely leaved and spiny, their elegant glossy foliage deepens in winter to a dark green suffused with bronze.

The warty barberry, *Berberis verruculosa*, grows in a neat low mound to about three feet (my bush is two feet high by three feet wide), making it an ideal evergreen for the small garden. Its pale green arching branches are densely clothed with clusters of small, very narrow leaves, edged in tiny prickles, that are a deep shiny green above and chalky white

WARTY BARBERRY
(Berberis verruculosa)

on their undersides. Between the clusters of leaves, formidable cream-colored spines jut out dramatically from the barberry's stems. In November there is an occasional flash of scarlet among the leaves, and where they join together in clusters along the branches there is also a daub of red. My young bush has yet to produce any berries. Donald Wyman describes them as "violet-black . . . covered with a grayish bloom." He goes on to say that this small shrub "could be considered one of the best of the evergreen barberries for ornamental use."

I was introduced to *Berberis* × *gladwynensis* 'William Penn' on a visit to Wave Hill, that treasure chest of a garden above the Hudson, and I thought it the most attractive barberry I had ever seen. Admittedly, my knowledge of barberries is negligible. (I am familiar with a mere handful of kinds, while Wyman speaks of 120 varieties growing at the Arnold Arboretum.) Nonetheless it is a beautiful plant. Michael Dirr goes so far as to say (in his *Manual of Woody Landscape Plants*) that "its foliage may be the handsomest of any evergreen barberry."

I now have a small specimen of my own, which has

survived several harsh winters, although I suspect that this Pennsylvania-bred barberry is only marginally hardy for me. It, too, has a low mounded habit and arching branches of leathery leaves that have a bronze sheen in winter. But these leaves are much bigger than those of the warty barberry and are oval in shape. They are edged with numerous small prickles and interspersed with long impressive spines of the same bleached yellow. (Needless to say, the deer are not tempted to munch on these evergreens.)

Sprigs of these barberries, cut now and brought indoors, are an unusual and striking mantel decoration mixed with pinecones and berries and the soft green of juniper and pine boughs.

KEEPING
WARM
AT THE
BARN

A blustery wind has brought a change in the weather — an arctic chill has settled on Duck Hill. Our fingers and toes are quickly numbed by the stinging cold, and walks with the dogs are mercifully short and brisk.

The water buckets up at the barn are frozen and must be emptied and refilled several times a day. The ducks tuck their beaks under their wings (do their beaks get particularly cold?), and the barn cats sit crouched in the sun by the sheltered south ell of the barn. They are all puffed up like winter birds against the cold, their front paws tucked close to their chests and their tails wrapped neatly around their legs as if to keep out any drafts. The chickens, too, huddle here in the sun or busy themselves scratching for bugs in the comparative warmth of the horses' stalls.

Our comical little English game cock has mastered the problem of keeping warm at night. He waits until the big fat hens are lined up and already dozing on their roost, and then he squeezes himself in between two of them so that he is barely visible, warmly smothered in feathers.

VIEWS
FROM
INDOORS

When planning the garden, it is a good idea, I think, to keep in mind the views that are framed by the windows indoors. In our northern states, where temperatures can hover close to (or below) zero for days — sometimes weeks — at a time, and wind, sleet, and ice often make strolling outdoors unthinkable, much of our time in winter is spent viewing the garden from indoors. There are times, too, when, regardless of the weather, we are forced to remain inside because of chores that need to be done. In either case, it is nice to be consoled by a pleasant view through a window.

If we are lucky, a few appealing scenes will already exist. But we can also create a picture that will give us pleasure to see from indoors. It can be simply a small graceful tree planted just beyond the window, or a favorite statue sited at the far end of a lawn, or something more involved, like a series of clipped evergreens set in a pattern or a knot of herbs.

The western wall of our kitchen is mostly windows — two French doors, really, and a long matching window on each side — and these nicely frame the herb garden, which rises just above the terrace outside. The sundial, wound with ivy, is the garden's centerpiece, with the arbor beyond, and round bushes of boxwood mark the central path. At all times of year, this is an attractive prospect from the kitchen, and glimpses of it can be caught as you enter the house from the opposite end.

Many kitchens have a window just above the sink (ours, alas, does not), and since a good deal of our time is spent tediously washing dishes, this seems a natural spot from which to have an interesting view. (An especially ornamental shrub or tree supporting a frequently visited bird feeder would be one easily created and rewarding scene.)

One of my favorite Duck Hill views from indoors is an accident of nature. From several upstairs bedroom windows looking west, our oldest tree is beautifully framed. It is an immense white ash standing alone along the tumbling stone wall that edges our property beyond the barn. Its huge trunk is deeply furrowed, and its branches rise up dramatically toward the sky before finally spraying outward to form the crown. Behind the great ash lies a field, just glimpsed from the windows, soft with long grass and warm-colored in winter. In the distance are rolling blue hills as far as the eye can see.

At the end of our new bedroom wing is a bay window, inside of which our bathtub is rather prominently placed. I soak there now gazing out at rubble and weeds. But I envision a small stone garden, protected and private, with a birdbath at its center, just opposite my tub, set on a pedestal high enough so that the ducks won't claim it for their own. Just beyond, a dry retaining wall will curve out in a small semicircle to echo the bay. Here, if there is enough sun, I will tuck in a wealth of rock plants, pinks and campanulas, saponaria and arabis. Above the wall there will be a graceful screen, white Persian lilacs, perhaps, or, better still, a low spreading Japanese snowbell tree. How nice to look up from my bath into branches of pendulous white bells in June.

JAPANESE SNOWBELL TREE
(Styrax japonica)

BIBLIOGRAPHY

INDEX

Bibliography

Bailey, Liberty H. *Hortus Third*. New York: Macmillan, 1976.

Barnes, Don. *Daffodils: For Home, Garden and Show*. Portland, Oreg.: Timber Press, 1987.

Beales, Peter. *Classic Roses*. London: Collins Harvill, 1985.

Bowles, E. A. *My Garden in Spring*. 1914. Reprint. Pawlet, Vt.: Theophrastus, 1971.

Clausen, Ruth Rogers, and Nicolas Ekstrom. *Perennials for American Gardens*. New York: Random House, 1989.

Dana, Mrs. William Starr. *How to Know the Wild Flowers*. 1893. Reprint. Boston: Houghton Mifflin, 1989.

Dirr, Michael A. *Manual of Woody Landscape Plants*. 3rd ed. Champaign, Ill.: Stipes, 1975.

Fogg, John M., Jr. *Weeds of Lawn and Garden*. Philadelphia: University of Pennsylvania Press, 1945.

Foster, Gertrude B. *Herbs for Every Garden*. Rev. ed. New York: E. P. Dutton, 1973.

Fox, Helen Morgenthau. *Gardening with Herbs for Flavor and Fragrance*. New York: Macmillan, 1934.

Genders, Roy. *Miniature Bulbs*. New York: St. Martin's Press, 1963.

Gerard, John. *The Herbal or General History of Plants*. 1633. Reprint. New York: Dover, 1975.

Grieve, Mrs. M. *A Modern Herbal*. 1931. Reprint. New York: Dover, 1971.

Hole, S. Reynolds. *A Book about Roses*. London: Thomas Nelson & Sons, 1901.

Jekyll, Gertrude. *Children and Gardens*. New ed. London: Country Life, 1934.

———. *Colour Schemes for the Flower Garden*. 1908. Reprint. Suffolk: Antique Collectors' Club, 1982.

———. *Home and Garden*. London: Longmans, Green, 1900.

———. *Roses for English Gardens*. 1902. Reprint. Suffolk: Antique Collectors' Club, 1982.

———. *Wood and Garden*. 1899. Reprint. London: Longmans, Green, 1914.

Jekyll, Gertrude, and George S. Elgood. *Some English Gardens*. 1904. New ed. London: Longmans, Green, 1920.

Lacy, Allen. *The Garden in Autumn*. New York: Atlantic Monthly Press, 1990.

Lloyd, Christopher. *The Well-Chosen Garden*. New York: Harper & Row, 1984.

———. *The Year at Great Dixter*. New York: Viking, 1987.

McGourty, Frederick. *The Perennial Gardener*. Boston: Houghton Mifflin, 1989.

Mitchell, Henry. *The Essential Earthman*. Bloomington: Indiana University Press, 1981.

Page, Russell. *The Education of a Gardener*. London: Collins, 1962.

Rickett, Harold William. *Wild Flowers of the United States*. Vol 1. New York: McGraw Hill, 1965.

Rohde, Eleanour Sinclair. *Herbs and Herb Gardening*. London: Media Society, 1936.

Scott-James, Anne. *Sissinghurst: The Making of a Garden*. London: Michael Joseph, 1978.

Strong, Roy. *Creating Formal Gardens*. Boston: Little, Brown, 1989.

Thomas, Graham Stuart. *Climbing Roses Old and New*. Rev. ed. London: Dent & Sons, 1978.

———. *Perennial Garden Plants*. London: Dent & Sons, 1976.

———. *The Old Shrub Roses*. Rev. ed. London: Dent & Sons, 1978.

———. *Shrub Roses of Today*. Rev. ed. London: Dent & Sons, 1974.

Wilder, Louise Beebe. *Colour in My Garden*. New York: Doubleday, 1918.

———. *The Fragrant Path*. New York: Macmillan, 1936.

———. *Hardy Bulbs*. 1936. Reprint. New York: Dover, 1974.

———. *My Garden*. New York: Doubleday, 1916.

Wilson, E. H. *Aristocrats of the Garden*. Boston: Stratford, 1926.

Wilson, Helen Van Pelt. *The Joy of Geraniums*. New York: William Morrow, 1972.

Wister, John C. *Bulbs for American Gardens*. Boston: Stratford, 1930.

Wyman, Donald. *Shrubs and Vines for American Gardens*. Rev. ed. New York: Macmillan, 1969.

———. *Trees for American Gardens*. New York: Macmillan, 1951.

———. *Wyman's Garden Encyclopedia*. Rev. ed. New York: Macmillan, 1977.

Index